# REDISCOVERING THE BRITISH EMPIRE

Edited by
Barry J. Ward

OPEN FORUM SERIES

KRIEGER PUBLISHING COMPANY
MALABAR, FLORIDA
2002

Original Edition 2002

Printed and Published by
**KRIEGER PUBLISHING COMPANY**
**KRIEGER DRIVE**
**MALABAR, FLORIDA 32950**



**Library of Congress Cataloging-in-Publication Data**

Rediscovering the British Empire / edited by Barry J. Ward.—Original ed.
p. cm. — (Open forum series)
Includes bibliographical references and index.
ISBN 1-57524-124-2 (alk. paper)
1. Great Britain—Colonies—History. I. Ward, Barry J., 1942– II. Series.

DA16 .R33 2002
909'.0971241—dc21

2001038668

10 9 8 7 6 5 4 3 2

# CONTENTS

# FOREWORD

This superb collection of essays pursues the theme of "rediscovering the British Empire" in the sense of reappraisal and reinterpretation based on new and original sources. Each chapter rests on vigorous empirical research, and each suggests trends in interpretation that have emerged within the last decade. The book offers perspective on the British imperial experience. We now live in a postcolonial as well as post-Cold War era. With the advantages of distance in time and access to archival and other sources, the historian can now study and reflect on the great events in the history of the European empires much more dispassionately than was possible during the era of decolonization.

It is useful to view the theme of "rediscovery" in relation to the transformation of the subject of the history of the British Empire in recent decades. Until about 1950 historians of British imperialism usually saw their discipline as part of the larger subject of British history. With the development of area studies in Asia and Africa, "imperial" history appeared to be disintegrating into its component parts. As these essays make clear, this was a myopic view. The history of the British Empire can only benefit from a larger vision of the subject that reconciles area studies with imperial history, as in the chapter by Sara Sohmer on Fiji, or that deals with literature and the place of the empire in the literary imagination, as in the chapter by Barry Ward on Joyce Cary. In reading the book as a whole, one particular issue captures the attention of the reader—the way in which the British imposed the cultural values of their own society on the different peoples in the empire, as is evident in Bruce Westrate's essay on reform in India. The implicit suggestion is that, just as the British tended to see the world through British eyes and to inquire whether "progress" was a reality or an illusion, so Americans in the twenty-first century continue to debate similar issues in relation to American power and America's place in the world.

The British Empire was a worldwide system of informal economic and political influence as well as a structure of direct colonial rule. This theme is prominent in the chapters by Richard Bradshaw on Japan and Theodore Vestal on Ethiopia. In quite different ways, and in different degrees of magnitude, both Japan and Ethiopia were important for the British imperial system. But in whatever way the empire is viewed, whether as a formal or informal structure, India was at the center of the British system as an empire in its own right and as an expansive force in the subcontinent. The two chapters by Mark Jacobsen and John Brobst on the "Great Game" of defending India and rationalizing the British presence in Asia provide one of the book's main themes. The Great Game is not over. The United States has now assumed some of the attributes of the old British Empire. Ethnic upheavals, the breakup of territorial and political units, and peace keeping in disturbed areas would have been quite familiar to the British in earlier eras. For the British, however, the Great Game came to an end with the collapse of their position in Aden in 1967, as is described in the chapter by John Allgood.

The essays in this book carry the reader into lively debates based on rigorous historical inquiry. They will be read with interest by those concerned not merely with the history of the British Empire but with the legacy of European imperialism. The essays were inspired by a summer seminar sponsored by the National Endowment for the Humanities. All of the contributors and I myself warmly thank the NEH for the seminar that led to the present book.

Wm. Roger Louis

# ACKNOWLEDGMENTS

This volume on rediscovering the British Empire owes its existence to a National Endowment for the Humanities seminar directed by W. Roger Louis at The University of Texas at Austin in 1996. Contributors to this volume wish to thank Professor Louis, Kerr Chair in English History and Culture and Editor-in-Chief of *The Oxford History of the British Empire*, and the NEH for providing the inspiration and opportunity for their efforts.

# ACKNOWLEDGMENTS

[illegible]

# CONTRIBUTORS

**John Allgood** completed his Ph.D. in history at The University of Texas at Austin in 1999. An independent scholar, he currently lives in Madison, Wisconsin.

**Richard Bradshaw** is assistant professor of history at Centre College in Kentucky. His teaching and publishing focus on Japan and European colonialism in Africa.

**Peter John Brobst** is assistant professor of history at Ohio University, where he teaches courses on modern Britain, the British Empire, and Middle East diplomacy. He has written *The Legacy of the Great Game: Sir Olaf Caroe, India's Independence, and World Power*, and is currently working on a study of Anglo-American sea power and strategy in the Indian Ocean between 1956 and 1976.

**Mark Jacobsen** is professor of military history at the USMC Command and Staff College, Quantico, Virginia. His doctoral dissertation written at the University of California, Irvine, deals with the Indian army during the interwar years.

**W. Roger Louis** is Kerr Chair in English History and Culture and Distinguished Teaching Professor at The University of Texas at Austin. He is editor-in-chief of *The Oxford History of the British Empire*.

**Sara H. Sohmer** teaches British history at Texas Christian University in Ft. Worth. Her research centers on the British Empire in the western Pacific, and she has written on colonial Fiji and the Anglican missionary movement in Melanesia.

**Theodore M. Vestal** is professor of political science at Oklahoma State University where he teaches courses in constitutional law. He is author of *Ethiopia: A Post-Cold War African State* (Praeger, 1999).

**Barry J. Ward** is associate professor of English at West Virginia University where he teaches courses in African and Indian literatures and in folklore. In addition to publishing articles in those fields, he has co-authored a book on traditional architecture and edited a composition text.

**Bruce Westrate** is associate professor of history at Indiana University South Bend. He is author of *The Arab Bureau: British Policy in the Middle East* (Penn State Press, 1992).

# INTRODUCTION

The importance of studying Britain's past has never been in serious dispute. What has been in play, however, is just how to go about this study, especially when considering Britain's worldwide imperial system. Until the 1950s and the rapid development of area studies, Anglocentric accounts dominated, tending to deemphasize such elements as Asian and African nationalism and resistance. Gradually imperial historians lost their place to other historians, economists, and political scientists who were inevitably influenced by the antiimperialism of the nationalist movements of the 1950s and 1960s. This volume is an effort to begin reconciling three perspectives: first, the imperial viewpoint that the British transformed the world into their own image; second, the revisionist approach that characterizes the history of the British Empire as essentially one of collaboration and interaction between the British and those they colonized; and third, postcolonial criticism that focuses on opposition to imperialism and western values.

Contributions to this volume attempt to advance our understanding of the pervasive impact of the British Empire on its participants, on subsequent events, and particularly on the processes of imperialism itself. Chapters present separate arguments within themselves, but taken as a whole they also give us persuasive evidence that renewed attention to empire issues is warranted. The theme of rediscovery has been interpreted broadly to include new interpretations of problems thought to be solved, second looks at issues in light of recent historiography, and interpretations drawing on nontraditional sources of evidence such as literature.

Fiji and issues of imperial expansion are Sara Sohmer's subjects. Most significantly, she describes the process involved in the British acquisition of a part of the world where pressing national interests could not be convincingly argued either in strategic or economic terms and when the "forward march of empire" was not yet universally acknowledged to be the national destiny. From the early 1840s to the establishment of British colonial authority in 1874, Europeans on the scene in Fiji variously depicted the islanders as hopelessly debased cannibals, souls to be brought to Christian truth, potential citizens of a unified state, and cultural remnants of a dead civilization to be expunged by the forces of progress. This chapter surveys the complex perceptions of Fijians "constructed" both for British colonial policymakers and the reading public by naval commanders, explorers, missionaries, travelers, and British officials in country. Sohmer masterfully examines various sources and constructs a unified picture of the pre-1874 period in Fiji. An example of New Imperialism emerges, one predating the period in which the necessity for and inevitability of empire were commonly voiced.

Studies of Anglo-Japanese relations in the period between the Meiji Restoration and the Second World War have focused on the convergence or conflict of British and Japanese interests in Asia. As Richard Bradshaw demonstrates, however, Japan had greater aspirations than to be a regional Asian power. She looked to British imperialism for her model. Bradshaw argues that Japanese perceptions of British imperialism in Africa had a dramatic impact during this period as Japan established strategic alliances, expanded trade, and entered into treaties. African markets became increasingly important to Japan after the First World War; at first they focused on trade with Egypt but soon had expanded their business activities all the way to the Cape. British erection of trade barriers in Africa in the 1930s, however, convinced the Japanese of the need to create an Asian Co-Prosperity Sphere free of such restrictions. Although after the Second World War the United States became Japan's role model, decades of earlier Japanese imperial policy can be understood as an imitation of, or reaction to, policies of the British Empire.

Why is present-day Ethiopia so beset with problems, especially in its relationships with Eritrea, Somalia, and the ethnic Amharas? In seeking an answer to this question, Theodore Vestal examines the impact on Ethiopia of British occupation during the Second World War. While characterizing The Federal Democratic Republic of Ethiopia as a troubled totalitarian state, an abuser of human rights, a thwarter of democratic processes, and a fomenter of ethnic distrust, Vestal nonetheless uncovers the roots of Ethiopia's problems, not only in Cold War and internal rivalries but also in British military occupation of the Horn of Africa which lasted from 1941–1952. Significant events occurring during the British administration are shown to be the source of much of the friction and distrust which continue to plague the region.

The British often turned to federation building to achieve their goals of maintaining hegemony in an area while at the same time moving it toward self-rule. Successful federations established in Canada, Australia, and South Africa preserved British predominance, whereas others, such as the Aden Federation, never delivered such a result. John Allgood discusses the attempt by Britain to establish the Aden Federation and the reasons for its ultimate failure. His detailed analysis of the situation in South Arabia gives readers a graphic example of how Britain attempted to preserve its influence and governmental structures in the period of decolonization and withdrawal, and, finally, how its failure in Aden has affected contemporary politics in the region.

The disintegration of the Soviet Union combined with the emergence of Chinese and Indian power have reopened discussion of what the Victorians called the "Great Game." In his chapter revisiting British/Russian competition in Central Asia, Mark Jacobsen examines the resumption of Great Game intrigue in Afghanistan from 1919 to 1939. Fears of a Soviet invasion of Afghanistan led Britain into elaborate planning for the defense of India, reminiscent on the surface of legendary nineteenth-century intrigues. That the threat of invasion turned out to be more imaginary than real is less important from an historical perspective than what British actions tell us about the state of empire between the wars.

Until recently it had been assumed that the Cold War had eclipsed the Great Game since global ascendancy no longer seemed to pivot on control of Eurasia's center. In his chapter on rediscovering the Great Game John Brobst presents a convincing case for the continuity between the strategies and tactics of the nineteenth-century British Empire and those of current post-Cold War policymakers. Brobst describes how South Asia was a focal point for world power conflicts long before British control of India or the Cold War, and how essential it is for us to recognize the Great Game as "an enduring model of Asian geopolitics."

Using novelist Joyce Cary's controversial *Mister Johnson* as a model, I attempt to demonstrate how this work of western literature set in a colonial environment can be used to explicate everyday operations and policies of colonial Britain. Cary's novel, set in early twentieth-century Nigeria, dramatizes the building of colonial infrastructure, in this case roads, and the effects on West African culture of British colonialism and western technology. Cary's Nigerian field notes and reports as well as official directives on the use of indigenous labor are employed to enhance textual analysis.

Bruce Westrate investigates a 170-year-old imperial controversy in order to comment on contemporary cultural debates. His chapter reexamines the controversy over Lord William Bentinck's 1829 abolition of *sati* (widow-burning) in British India. In the two decades predating Bentinck's appointment as governor-general, evangelical and liberal theorists had moved the East India Company to interventionist policies. Hinduism was challenged as missionaries increased efforts to convert Indians to Christianity. Religious rituals and social customs offensive to the British were prohibited on the grounds that such practices were morally repugnant and obstacles to progress. Bentinck's abolition of sati and his efforts to eliminate murder and robbery by the Thugs, followers of the god Kali, extended imperial intrusion into the practices of indigenous cultures and demarcated new limits of British tolerance for controversial behaviors. Westrate maintains that the controversy and subsequent debate over Bentinck's decisions provided further rationale for the eventual introduction of westernizing reforms involving education, social justice, and law. The sati debate raises questions of cultural relativism and multiculturalism that presage our own ongoing culture wars and international conflicts. Enlightenment concepts such as the preeminence of individual rights and democratic rule articulated by British imperialists and furthered by their American counterparts have been incorporated into the United Nations's Charter and are widely touted as the only reasonable bases upon which to found a society. Still, China, much of the Muslim world, and indeed India have a decidedly different definition of what constitutes a just society and a moral life. Battles over domestic social policy and government intervention in citizens' private lives are not unique to our era.

Justifications abound for a reexamination of the British Empire. Among the most important are the insights empire studies provide into the larger issues of power relations, cultural conflicts, religious disputes, and globalization of the world economy. For Americans who have struggled to understand the Cold War with the Soviet Union and who seek to define the United States's role as a superpower in the new century, the history of the British Empire provides invaluable lessons. The British Empire provides a fundamental key to understanding current American hegemony because, as Keith Booker has noted,

> . . . twentieth-century American history and twentieth-century British imperial history are not separable phenomena but part of the same sweeping global narrative, a fact that can be seen not only in the relatively direct replacement of British by American power in numerous former colonial settings but in the remarkable genealogical relationship between the

> rhetoric of American foreign policy in recent decades and the rhetoric of British imperialism in the century before that. (186)

This understanding does depend, of course, on what one means by "empire." With globalization "empire" has increasingly become economic and cultural although certainly the political and military manifestations remain significant.

American imperial power, projected just as often through economic/trade policies and through the power of television, movies and now the Internet, as through direct military intervention, is no less effective than was that of the British Empire. Since American economic and cultural power is also supported by a massive military capability that is being used with increasing frequency, it comes as little surprise that those affected by such power are striking back. Iraqi defiance of U.N. (read U.S.A.) directives is just the most publicized variety of such resistance. More ominous than Iraqi defiance and of more importance in the twenty-first century are the terrorist acts which now occur with greater frequency against Americans. Guided missile strikes no matter how accurate will not solve the problem of terrorism nor will simple-minded demonization of America's adversaries. American policymakers would do well to study the reasons for unrest and disquiet of formerly colonized peoples. The American Empire may yet discover in the history of British imperialism at least some of the lessons to be learned.

For an interpretation of the rise of the British Empire as inseparable from the rise of bourgeois power see M. Keith Booker, *Colonial Power, Colonial Texts* (Ann Arbor: Univ. of Michigan Press, 1997).

# 1

# SAVAGES, IMPERILED SOULS, AND CONSTITUTIONAL MONARCHIES: CHANGING PERCEPTIONS OF WORTH AND POWER IN PRECOLONIAL FIJI

**Sara H. Sohmer**

In his five-year tenure [1875–1880] as the first British governor of the crown colony of Fiji, Sir Arthur Hamilton Gordon initiated political, social, and economic policies that prevailed in the island colony until independence in 1970 and which, in the view of some scholars, continue to shadow the postcolonial era.[1] Gordon made the protection of the interests of Fiji's indigenous population the cornerstone of his colonial system. He hoped to secure Fijian rights to the land, forestall "premature" involvement by Fijians with the colony's money economy, and maintain customary practice through the authority of traditional chiefs. Although Gordon had to consider the demands of a resident European population of merchants and planters and the Colonial Office's insistence that the colony pay its own way, he tailored his responses to his particular, protective sense of the British imperial mission in Fiji. Because annexation and the Gordon years represent an obvious point of departure, scholars of nineteenth-century Fiji have quite reasonably focused most of their critical attention on Gordon's system, particularly since it survived all attempts at revision and became a permanent feature of the colonial landscape.[2]

But Fiji was not a blank slate for Great Britain in 1874. For almost forty years prior to the establishment of the crown colony, the missions, naval and exploring expeditions, and commerce that constituted a much expanded European presence in the western Pacific provided information about a region previously little known and seldom visited. Gordon's vision of colonial rule needs to be understood in the context of these earlier decades of contact—years in which British responses to Fijians and their culture ranged from fearful respect and horrified fascination to cautious optimism and arrogant disdain. These attitudinal shifts reflect both changes in the relative balance of power between Fijians and British subjects in Fiji itself and changing priorities in the home government's sense of imperial mission in the Pacific.

## REPORTING SAVAGES, REPORTING SOULS

Viewed from this expanded perspective, Gordon's insistence on the protection of Fijian interests has a certain irony. For most of Fiji's postcontact history, it was Europeans who found their interests and indeed their lives in need of protection from Fiji's dangerous waters and its even more dangerous inhabitants. Able Tasman in fact depicted the first European encounter with Fiji in 1643 in such negative terms that navigators studiously avoided the group for 130 years. The increased European contact that became possible with the appearance of reliable charts after Cook's partial survey in 1774 and the work of the United States Exploring Expedition in 1840 only enhanced Fiji's reputation for fierceness. If other island chains of the Pacific acquired benign European names with the voyages of discovery and exploration (e.g., the Societies, the Friendly Islands, the Sandwich Islands), Fiji, significantly, found its place on charts and maps as the Cannibal Islands.

Its reputation notwithstanding, by the early decades of the nineteenth century potential profits from the sandalwood and beche-de-mer[3] trades lured more ships to the islands, and a few Europeans found a permanent, if precarious, place for themselves. Traders, beachcombers, and, later, missionaries all survived in Fiji with the sufferance of powerful Fijian traditional leaders who found them useful for their own purposes. A beche-de-mer cargo could, in 1840, bring in $25,000 after a six-month voyage with fairly minimal overhead costs,[4] but absent a wage economy no trader could acquire this profitable commodity without the cooperation of a Fijian who could command the necessary labor involved.[5] In these circumstances, Fijians indisputedly held the whip hand. Cakobau, the war leader of Bau, was quite capable in the 1840s of collecting payment for a cargo in advance, defaulting on delivery, and threatening to eat dissatisfied clients.[6]

Even naval vessels had limited recourse in dealing with the exactions of Fijian chiefs. Charles Wilkes, the commander of the U.S. Exploring Expedition, had complied with demands for "port charges" when his expedition cruised the islands in 1840. Captain Belcher, the British commander of HMS *Sulphur*, however, took the position that Fijians had no real understanding of such things and refused to pay. Predictably, needed supplies were withheld and the ship's crew harassed until payment was forthcoming. Not only did Fijians understand trade and fees, Wilkes reported, but " . . . also the power they had in their hands of compelling the visitor to pay."[7]

Despite their insignificant numbers and their lack of ability to affect the outcome of particular interactions with Fijians, this resident and itinerant European population, most of whom were either British or American, did contrive to make Fiji more dangerous than ever. The introduction of firearms through trade and the presence of even a minuscule number of Europeans willing to act as advisors to warring chiefs completely changed the dimensions of Fijian warfare. For successful exploiters of new trade opportunities and new weapons technology, the complete subjugation of traditional enemies became a tempting possibility.[8]

Captain John Erskine, RN, basing his observation on his 1849 voyage, believed that the activities of Europeans " . . . free from all restraints of civilized life" in Fijian service were directly responsible for a decline in the Fijian population.[9] The Wesleyan missionary, Thomas Williams, who spent thirteen years in Fiji in the 1840s and 1850s, recognized the ritualized and limited nature of traditional warfare. Under contemporary conditions, however, he estimated the deaths in battle ran somewhere between 1500–2000 annually, without counting the additional decimation of wives strangled to "line the grave" of slain warriors.[10] Ratu Seru of Bau (later Cakobau), who because his home region enjoyed relative stability thanks to his father's longevity as chief of Bau, had a free hand to pursue his passion for war elsewhere. With the destructive resources now available, he shocked the islands with the vehemence of his attacks on neighboring districts. Following an attack on the Rewa district in 1845, he sacked and burned its chief town and personally directed the execution of the Rewa high chief. "War," he told a protesting missionary, "is the proper exercise of chiefs."[11] He might have added that in his own case, it was also a highly profitable exercise in terms of his place in the new trade economy of Fiji. By 1850 he had consolidated enough power through aggressive warfare for some Europeans to begin referring to him as Tui Viti or king of Fiji. Essentially meaningless in terms of

Fijian political reality, the spurious title nonetheless gave Cakobau greater access to the European goods critical to his imperial ventures.[12]

An expanded European presence in the 1840s and 1850s, in short, created a volatile climate in terms of disruption in the traditional balance of power, the breakdown of customary controls, and the changing scale of warfare brought about by the use of guns as items of trade. Significantly, these turbulent years also marked the appearance of the first extensive accounts of the islands available to British and American readers. In the introduction to his own *Fiji and the Fijians* published in 1859, the Wesleyan missionary Thomas Williams referred his readers to five other books with "useful information" on Fiji: Charles Wilkes's (USN) *Narrative of the United States Exploring Expedition* (1845); Captain John E. Erskine's (RN) *Journal of a Cruise Among the Islands of the Western Pacific* (1853); Mrs. Mary Wallis's *Life in Feejee or Five Years Among the Cannibals by a Lady* (1851); Rev. Walter Lawry's *First and Second Missionary Visits to the Friendly and Feejee Islands*; and Rev. Robert Young's *Journal of a Deputation to the Southern World* (1855).[13] Observers of the Fijian scene in these years might logically be expected to record the dangerous and uncertain atmosphere as well as the discrepancy in balance of power between themselves and Fijians. But even the most measured and circumspect of those who wrote about Fiji appear to have been shocked to the core by the violence they witnessed. The heart of their repugnance was, not surprisingly, cannibalism.

The scholarly debate on the place and function and indeed the actual existence of cannibalism has been volatile and is likely to remain so.[14] There can be little doubt, however, that the nineteenth-century writers who "reported" Fiji to the European reading public were convinced of its prominent place in Fijian life and spared their readers nothing in their documentation of its horrors. Wilkes, the scientific observer, devoted most of his narrative to descriptions of Fiji's physical features, its flora and fauna, and the material culture of the islanders. In the best tradition of scientific illustration, the engravings accompanying the text were meticulously detailed. The Fijians depicted were given European features with an exotic cast, but there was no attempt to make them particularly savage or threatening. But when Wilkes described particular aspects of Fijian custom, he abandoned any pretense of detachment. While recognizing that cannibalism had its probable origins in the ritualized context of sacrifice, Wilkes, relying on eye-witness accounts, believed that contemporary practice had moved into the realm of habit and preference.[15] Religious sacrifices had become more frequent as a means of indulging an acquired taste, and human flesh had become a status gift to be sent to those one wished to impress. One chief, Wilkes wrote, made a point of sending a human as his share of a feast when only a pig was requested. Bodies of enemies killed in battle were always eaten, but raids on noncombatants, purchase, and sacrifice all served the apparently insatiable demand. And while Wilkes believed human flesh was reserved for men, he found no privileged categories when it came to victims. Women and children were indeed preferred as a matter of taste, and relatives and friends, in particular circumstances, might also be consumed.[16]

Wilkes was equally offended by such practices as wife-strangling, premature burial of the still-viable sick and elderly, and the human sacrifices required to build the great war canoes.[17] Impressed as he was with the heroic lives of the few Wesleyan missionaries in Fiji, he came to the conclusion that their only hope of success lay in removing Fijian children from a culture " . . . degraded beyond the conception of civilized people" and starting anew.[18] He counted himself fortunate to leave the Cannibal Islands with the loss of only two members of the expedition, men later honored by a monument bearing witness that they " . . . fell by the hands of savages, while promoting the cause of science and philanthropy."[19]

Other accounts available to British and American readers echoed Wilkes's sense of horror. Mrs. Mary Wallis, an American married to a sea captain engaged in the beche-de-mer trade, presented Fijians as " . . . a deeply degraded people" who fried child victims of cannibalism and rewarded their own children with cooked hands to gnaw. Her account described wife-strangling, premature burials, and the details of tortures inflicted on those unfortunate enough to be captured during warfare.[20] Thomas Williams, whose 1859 account has been adjudged the best source on early Fiji by later scholars,[21] also detailed torture, human sacrifices, and the butchering of corpses for cooking. "Cannibalism," he wrote, "is one of the elements of society; it forms one of their pursuits and is regarded by the mass as a refinement."[22] One Rev. M. Russell, whose 1853 second-hand account did not make Williams's list, included a mariner's report of a cannibal feast of suspicious symmetry featuring 200 pigs, 200 baskets of yams, 200 fowls, and 200 baked humans. If Russell's evidence is suspect, there can be little quarrel with his tropes. The requisite stories of wife-strangling and premature burials follow cannibal tales in short order.[23]

Even Captain Erskine, perhaps the least sensational of writers about Fiji in this period, listed all of the reliable reports of cannibalism he knew and provided more specific detail on cooking and taste preferences. He reiterated Wilkes's impression of the scale of modern practice, however, and suggested that the Fijian case should be viewed in some sort of comparative context. The European historical record contained numerous reported incidents of cannibalism and no evidence that all Europeans were instinctively repulsed by the practice.[24]

Ironically, many of the same accounts that sensationalized Fijian cultural practice also introduced one of the other major elements in British and American perceptions of precolonial Fiji—the possibility of the transformation of the savage heathen. Wesleyan missionaries arrived in Fiji from Tonga in 1835 determined to bring an end to the dichotomy between the paradisiacal appearance of the islands and the ferocity of their inhabitants. Their numbers were always small in this period, and for years they were tolerated only because they could be useful in facilitating the chiefs' interchange with visiting ships. But when Cakobau, for reasons that had at least as much to do with statecraft as spiritual enlightenment, made the decision to *lotu* (convert) in 1854 the missionaries' way was considerably smoothed. By 1858, Thomas Williams could report a church membership of 7,000 Fijians with another 2,000 on trial for membership and "stated listeners" numbering 60,000.[25]

The missionaries' own accounts and those of others sympathetic to their cause contained the basis of a cautiously positive image of Fijians. Cannibals and wife-stranglers were clearly not well cast as noble savages, and no one writing in this period, as we have seen, shied away from presenting Fijians in the worst possible light. But Fijians, if "deeply degraded" might also be "long neglected," the ". . . the Ishmaelites of the South Pacific."[26] If Fijians could be changed, the very depths of their degradation (especially if set against the backdrop of a tropical paradise) could only dramatize the transforming power of the missionaries' message. For that transformation to take place Fijians needed to be credited with at least some redeeming features and basic humanity.

Erskine found Fijians, for all their obvious faults, energetic, courageous, and manly in comparison with the inhabitants of other Pacific island groups and not without their admirers among "respectable" Europeans who knew them. "It must not be inferred, from the slowness of the missionaries' progress among some of the tribes," he wrote, "that the people are incapable of ultimate civilization."[27] Williams in turn focused attention on Fijians as settled agriculturalists. Fijian men gardened with meticulous care, growing a greater variety of local food crops than were to be found elsewhere in the Pacific. Moreover, they had quickly adapted newly introduced plants such as tobacco to their own needs. He also saw Fijians as skilled builders and craftsmen, noting in detail the complexities of Fijian buildings and canoes. As much as he deplored Fijian warfare, he conceded he had witnessed incidents of bravery and intelligence among Fijian warriors.[28]

But the real case for Fijian potential according to Williams was to be found in the Fijian transformed by the Christian faith. In 1845, an important chief and thoroughgoing cannibal, Verani of Viwa, made the *lotu* and promptly gave up fighting, to the great disgust of his former ally, Cakobau. Williams recorded Verani's eloquent prayers for his readers:

> When our minds think of Fiji, they are greatly pained, for the men and women of Fiji are Thy people and these Thy people are strangled and clubbed and destroyed . . . set us in motion that we may not be so useless as we have been; but that we may now for the time to come live to extend Thy kingdom that it may reach all Fiji.[29]

The theme of Fijian transformation can be matched in many of these accounts with the presentation of the heroic struggles of the missionaries themselves. Mrs. Wallis's description of the death in 1848 of the missionary Hunt who had supplied Wilkes with eyewitness accounts of cannibalism provided a missionary parallel of the sentiments expressed by Verani. With his dying breath Hunt exclaimed, "Oh, let me pray once more for Feejee! . . . Oh, for one more baptism!"[30] Erskine provided an even more dramatic example of missionary heroism in his account of Mrs. Lyth and Mrs. Calvert who, apprised of a cannibal feast in progress while their husbands were away, sailed off on their own to face down cannibal chiefs and successfully rescued three women designated for the baking pits.[31] Surely it could be hoped that the people for whom so much had been willingly sacrificed by dedicated missionaries and who themselves showed signs of finally responding to the missionary message might continue to progress. Perhaps Fijians, unlike the indigenous inhabitants of Australia, need not be written off completely. They were not, wrote Captain Erskine, in fact without those " . . . qualities which excite the admiration and attachment of more civilized races."[32]

## FIJI AND THE OFFICIAL MIND

The ambivalence of European observers towards Fijians and their culture was thus well established by 1860 when the British government found itself drawn into greater direct involvement in the area. From 1860 to the acquisition of Fiji in 1874, British policy on Fiji revealed much the same ambivalence regarding the character of Fijians and their place in their own islands. To the extent that it concerned itself with Fiji at all, official Britain appears to have initially shared a relatively optimistic view of Fijians and their culture. In 1853 the governor of New South Wales commissioned Charles St. Julian, a Sydney journalist, to make recommendations concerning the precise nature of any British presence in Fiji. St. Julian concluded that British naval commanders might advise and assist native rulers in constructing sound governing principles *when asked* but should otherwise avoid interfering. His other recommendation, the naming of a British consul, was adopted by the Foreign Office, and the first consul, W. T. Pritchard, was appointed in 1856.[33] Pritchard, however, took a far more proactive approach to Fiji than the Foreign Office had envisioned. The consequences of his initiatives provide insight into the range of official perspectives on this remote part of the world prior to the Cession of 1874.

In 1858, acting entirely on his own initiative, Pritchard persuaded the most successful Fijian exploiter of the opportunities created by trade and new weapons technology, Cakobau, to extend an offer of cession of the islands to Great Britain. The language of the cession offer of 1858 was almost certainly Pritchard's. It proclaimed Cakobau as the sole sovereign of Fiji, so recognized by Great Britain, France, and the United States, with exclusive authority to transfer sovereignty to Great Britain in return for its assumption of a debt of $45,000 owed the United States for damages to the U.S. consul's property by some of Cakobau's "subjects."[34] In consideration for the retirement of this debt, 200,000 acres of land was to be made over to the British Crown in fee simple. Cakobau would retain the title of Tui Viti and the authority to rule the indigenous population.[35] The fact that Cakobau had never been recognized as sole sovereign by either Fijians or informed Europeans appears not to have troubled Pritchard.

When Pritchard sailed to England with the cession offer, he brought with him samples of sea island cotton grown in Fiji and visited, in turn, the Foreign Office, Exeter Hall, and the Manchester Cotton Supply Association. The latter obligingly supplied a resolution urging that " . . . the attention of Her Majesty's government ought to be directed to securing for this country the means of obtaining those supplies."[36] Perhaps for this reason, the Foreign Office passed the matter to the Colonial Office for consideration. The colonial secretary, the Duke of Newcastle, recognizing that very little of substance was known about Fiji, decided on an investigating commissioner as the best course of action. His appointee, Colonel William Smythe of the Royal Artillery, received explicit instructions to ascertain the nature of land ownership, the state of civilization (i.e., the degree to which cannibalism and other unacceptable practices had faded from the scene), the feasibility of agricultural development, and Fiji's suitability as a line station for rapid mail steamers from Australia to Panama.

All of this suggests an imperial scenario of classic proportions: the involvement of missionary interests, the development of a commodity needed by Britain in a controlled setting, a *fait accompli* generated by an individual on the scene, control of key points in Britain's communications and shipping network. Only security interests and national honor—matters Newcastle specifically excluded from the scope of Smythe's inquiry—are missing from the mix.[37]

In fact, none of the considerations involved in the 1858 offer proved compelling. Smythe spent ten months in Fiji interviewing Fijian chiefs from every district of the islands and the resident European community. He found little to be as Pritchard had represented it, and he reported as much to the colonial secretary. Less dangerous, shorter mail routes were to be had on a line farther south. Cotton seemed to do well, but neither the land nor the labor force it required was available. Wesleyan missionaries resident in the islands for years assured him that Cakobau had never been recognized as the king of Fiji and was only one of several independent, influential chiefs. The land he had earmarked to be conveyed to the British Crown lay in areas he neither owned nor controlled. Land in general appeared to be vested in families rather than individuals, and its alienation therefore became a very complex matter.

All things considered, Smythe was of the opinion that " . . . it would not be expedient that Her Majesty's Government should accept the offer which has been made."[38] The cession would not serve any imperial purpose that Smythe could foresee and could prove expensive. Nor could it be established that Fijians would benefit, however tempting the prospect of the extension of civilization and the suppression of remaining barbaric practice might be. Smythe concluded that the welfare of the islanders would be best secured by a native government advised by Europeans. The most the British government should consider was the extension of magisterial powers to the consul for the purpose of controlling renegade British subjects.[39] Smythe's recommendations were accepted. Pritchard found himself dismissed.[40]

Smythe's views on the role of native government are of particular interest in view of the parliamentary debate between 1872 and 1874 over the acquisition of Fiji. The inability of Fijians to order themselves and the fate of the European community figured prominently in proannexation arguments. Yet Smythe in 1860 found the native government the best vehicle for insuring the well-being of islanders, a view that became the de facto British policy on Fiji until 1872. Fijians might be problematic given their recent history,[41] but the concept of Fijian potential developed by earlier observers in the context of the Christian transformation had, by 1860, been expanded to include the possibility of self-government.

Smythe's assessment was almost certainly based both on his own observations in Fiji and his understanding of the political realities of the Pacific at mid-century. The island peoples of the Pacific from the last quarter of the eighteenth century shared a common necessity: the reordering of traditional society to meet the challenges presented by an intrusive European presence. By 1850, the Pomares of Tahiti, the Kamehamehas of Hawaii, and the Taufa'ahau in Tonga had successfully used customary strategies and the new resources of western technology and expertise to create centralized governments with at least the trappings of constitutional monarchy. The effectiveness of these native governments, their impact on traditional culture, and the degree to which they were the creations of European advisors continue to be a source of debate.[42] Neither the Hawaiian nor the Tahitian monarchy survived the "scramble for the Pacific" that characterized the later decades of the century, and Tonga retained its monarchy only in combination with its status as a British protectorate. But in the 1860s the three Polynesian societies provided viable examples of what an island government might be. Smythe saw no reason why Fijians might not follow a similar development. And indeed Fijians and resident Europeans made several attempts to establish such a native government in the years between 1860 and 1874.

Fiji, however, was not Polynesia. Part of the difficulty lay in traditional social and political practice in Fiji.[43] While Fiji, like its Polynesian neighbors, had a hierarchical social structure, its political order was comparatively fluid with competing chiefs depending on personal shrewdness and prowess in battle to consolidate their power. Nor could any proposed centralized native government in Fiji rely on established patterns of unity and consolidated power as was the case in the Polynesian kingdoms. The first such government, the Confederation of Chiefs, was created in 1865 with the guidance of the second British consul in Fiji, H. M. Jones. Anxious to have recourse to a body with the authority to conclude treaties with the British, Jones invited seven of the most important chiefs to form some sort of government. The chiefs readily agreed to meet annually and promised to compile a uniform set of laws for Fiji. They elected Cakobau president, adopted a flag, and in general appeared to be on the track Jones wanted. In short order, however, conflicts developed among the chiefs, and the experiment with native government on a national scale came to nothing. On a regional level, experiments in native government in the 1860s enjoyed more success. Chief Vakawaletabua in Bau and the expatriate Tongan chief Ma'afu in the Lau group headed regional governments that maintained law and order and regulated the land sales to foreigners who constituted a growing problem in Fiji. The regional kingdom of Bau that the Europeans around Cakobau set up in his name in 1867, however, proved to be no better than Jones's effort. Despite a showy "coronation for Cakobau and the formulation of a constitution modeled on that of Hawaii, the kingdom of Bau never really functioned."[44]

Whatever the incompatibilities of these experiments in western-style government and Fijian tradition, the real difficulty for the development of an indigenous national government in Fiji must be tied to the escalation of European interests in the islands. The rising price of cotton following the outbreak of the Civil War in the United States generated new interest in Fiji from Australia and New Zealand. The British consul's commercial reports, while not totally reliable, give some idea of the changes in the scale of commerce between 1863 and 1870. Trading in some traditional commodities such as beche-de-mer ended altogether in these years. Coconut oil, another market commodity produced by Fijians, dropped from a value of £9,900 in 1863 to £4,950 by 1870. Cotton, by contrast, went from a value £400 to £92,700 on the world market in the same decade.[45] In 1867 thirty bales of Fijian cotton sold in Liverpool for £65 per bale, and the rush to Fiji from Australia and New Zealand was on.[46] The commodities that held the most promise of profit were, in short, no longer those in which Fijians figured as suppliers or producers.[47]

Aside from the problem of the sheer numbers of Europeans that Fiji had to absorb in these years, the character of these new settlers bore little resemblance to the seamen, missionaries, traders, naval officers, and consuls who had previously shaped British thinking about the islands.[48] For some older residents, the new wave represented little more than a "semicriminal class" escaping economic depression in New Zealand and Australia.[49] Even without so harsh a judgment, the new settlers were for the most part young men possessed of only the limited capital cotton cultivation required and who identified, not with Great Britain, but with the colonial societies of the Antipodes. The political culture that had evolved in these colonies of settlement by the last third of the nineteenth century valued democratic rights for white Europeans and characteristically challenged traditional concepts of authority and custom.[50] Their relationship with indigenous populations was primarily one of displacement and conquest, now lent a gloss of intellectual respectability by Social Darwinism. Nothing in the experience of these new settlers, in short, boded well for a view of their place in Fiji as anything other than dominant. The goal of any Fijian government should be, wrote one settler, " . . . to obtain such a constitution as will secure to the white race that preeminence in the government of the country to which it is entitled by intellect and civilization. . . . We shall gradually extend our dominion over the countless islands, whose useless luxuriance is awaiting the advent of our race, to be converted into beneficial fertility, and whose savage inhabitants we shall teach the divine religion of work."[51] Thus, from the beginning of the cotton-planting boom to the Cession of 1874, long-term European residents content with some system of native government found themselves at odds with new settlers imbued both with the limited democratic principles and the racism of the colonial societies from which they came. From the point of view of the newcomers, purchase of land in Fiji carried with it a separate sovereignty, the sovereignty of civilized men among savages.[52]

Neither old nor new settlers nor Fijians, however, could dispute the need for renewed efforts at establishing some sort of government by 1870. The settlers, although they seem for the most part to have expected that Fijians would eventually "vacate" the land in the same manner as Australian Aborigines or the Maori of New Zealand, remained decidedly vulnerable in a Fiji where the "vanishing natives" still numbered 140,000. The British consul could take limited action only in cases involving British subjects, and that amounted to little more than registering titles from land purchases from Fijians and requesting a ship or two of the royal navy stand by in case of major threats to settlers. Fijian leaders such as Cakobau who had historically been able to turn European interests to their own advantage found themselves less and less able to do so and had developed deep reservations about the motives and attitudes of the planter population.[53]

Early in 1871 a group of established merchants approached Cakobau, proposing that he head a constitutional monarchy that would serve both European and Fijian interests equally. Cakobau saw in the proposal a chance of consolidating the support of the chiefs and regaining some control over events. He successfully solicited Fijian support for the new government and found rather unconventional financing for its initial expenditures.[54] By the fall of 1871, the new government had in place a monarch, a constitution, a privy council of chiefs and European ministers, and an elected assembly. For Cakobau and his ministers it must have seemed that another Pacific experiment in native or at least a mixed European/Fijian government had been established. And so it apparently seemed to Her Majesty's government. When queried about the situation in Fiji in February 1872, undersecretary of state for foreign affairs, Viscount Enfield, replied that so long as the new government in Fiji exercised actual authority Britain was prepared to deal with it as a de facto government, though formal recognition would have to wait until more information was in hand.[55]

Unfortunately for the principle of native government, it became increasingly difficult for the new government to exercise that authority. By the spring of 1872, the king's ministers and the legislative assembly had reached an impasse. Since it was assumed that Fijians were represented by the chiefs in the privy council and by the minister of native affairs, the legislative assembly was elected entirely by the settler community. Its interests reflected settler concerns to the exclusion of all else. The degree of contempt for Cakobau and Fijians shown on the floor of that house and in the editorial columns of Fiji's new newspaper, the *Fiji Times*, still astonishes. One member of the Assembly in July, 1872 proclaimed, "Is it not an insult to the House, and to every white man in the country to have an old nigger like the King set up, as he is being set up? King indeed . . . he would be more in his place digging or weeding a white man's garden."[56] The *Fiji Times*, which throughout the 1870s consistently defended planter interests, wrote in July 1873 when Cakobau dismissed the assembly and began governing with his ministers alone that,

> . . . the white settlers of Fiji . . . are today the ruling power of the group, and the chiefs and the natives are merely their puppets . . . Her (Fiji's) destiny is sealed and as surely as the American Indians, the New Zealanders, and the Australians have had to give way to the superior race, so surely must the Fijian follow the same course. Fiji must now become the home of a white race, its original inhabitants are no doubt doomed . . . Their inability to govern a people . . . must be apparent.[57]

By early in 1873, annexation by Great Britain had come to be seen in some parts of the settler community as the only viable solution for the protection of the interests of British subjects in Fiji. For the king's ministers, particularly John Bates Thurston who would later become the fourth governor of British Fiji, annexation seemed to offer the only possible way of providing any protection for Fijians given the rapacity of the settlers. Cakobau remained ambivalent, but the threat posed by the settlers to Fijian land finally persuaded him that he and his people had little choice but to be "slaves to England."[58]

## REDEFINING THE IMPERIAL MISSION

In Fiji itself, the relationship among the relative numbers of British subjects on the scene, the new emphasis on the acquisition of land by settlers,[59] the accelerated pace of change, and the problems of adapting Fijian patterns to western political patterns, and the diminished status assigned Fijians makes a fairly tidy equation. The response to the issue of Fiji and its people raised during the annexation debate in Great Britain is another matter. One of the most striking features of that debate is the manner in which Fijians *competent* and Fijians *deserving* become Fijians *irrelevant* to the issue. Ironically, this diminished concern for Fijians was driven by humanitarian concern for other Pacific islanders. Even before cession and rumors of cession engaged the attention of Parliament, questions involving Fiji had become conflated with the broader humanitarian issue of the Pacific Islands' labor trade.

This notorious trade in contract labor was itself a response to the development of labor-intensive commercial agriculture in the Pacific region in the 1860s and 1870s.[60] While there was little or no objection to the contract labor system per se, reports of abuses (kidnapping, fraudulent contracts, marginal living conditions) led organizations in Britain such as the Anti-Slavery Society and the Aborigine Protection Society to represent an unregulated trade as little more than a resurgence of a slave trade serving British possessions and perpetrated by British subjects.[61] Their campaign for protective, regulatory legislation moved forward in 1871 when islanders in the Santa Cruz group murdered the well-known Bishop of Melanesia, John C. Patteson, in retaliation for abuses suffered at the hands of labor traders. In 1872 Parliament passed the Pacific Islanders Protection Bill, creating a system of inspection and regulation for all ships engaged in the trade that served British possessions.[62] Fiji figured prominently in the labor trade as both a market for the labor needed to work its cotton plantations and as an important port for ships engaged in the trade. But as long as Fiji's government remained problematic, it lay outside the regulatory net. As this issue became the principal topic of discourse on the Pacific in Great Britain, Fijians, who had no status as victims of the trade and who could, through their failure to order Fiji, even be seen as complicit in it, largely ceased to be a focus of humanitarian concern.

From June 1872 until annexation in the fall of 1874, the pro-annexation party in Parliament was led by William McArthur (1809–1887), member for Lambeth, future Lord Mayor of London, and active supporter of the Aborigine Protection Society and the Wesleyan Missionary Society.[63] In McArthur's rhetorical excesses, the very well-being of the British Empire seemed to ride on these tiny islands in the South Pacific. Fiji, he argued, had tremendous economic potential; its sturdy, pioneering British subjects deserved protection; its strategic importance to the navy could not be disputed. The expense of having ships standing by to protect British subjects could be eliminated by annexing islands which could then be effectively ordered with only a gunboat or two. He consistently ridiculed the Cakobau government, except when he came to the cession offer, at which point that same government was transformed into a native authority requiring a respectful answer. Again and again, McArthur returned to the need to eliminate Fiji as a loophole in the regulation of the labor trade.[64] Conspicuously absent from his and all other proannexation representations of the Fiji question is any discussion of the place or the needs or the future of Fiji's indigenous inhabitants.

These arguments and the continuing deterioration of the Cakobau government eventually combined to persuade. The colonial secretary of the new Disraeli government, Lord Carnarvon, informed the House of Lords in July 1874, that given the numbers of English settlers, the weight of English capital invested, and general English involvement in the issue of peace in the islands " . . . it would not be safe to fold our arms and say we would not have anything to do with the Islands."[65] Great Britain would undertake the government of Fiji. But at the Cession of 1874 none of the perceptions of Fijians constructed in the precolonial period—powerful savages, transformed heathens, competent political actors, doomed impediments to a superior race, political incompetents—served to give them place or protection in their own land. Place and protection, value and worth in the new colonial order would require a new discourse and a new methodology. Charles Hamilton Gordon, Fiji's first British governor, would find that discourse in Victorian anthropology. His methodology was largely his own—the creation of a place for Fijians within a "ring fence"[66] of British-defined and British-protected traditions.

# REFERENCES

1. See Stephanie Lawson, "The Myth of Cultural Homogeneity and Its Implications for Chiefly Power and Politics in Fiji," *Comparative Studies in Society and History*, 32 (Oct. 1990), 795–821 for the connection between colonial instigation of traditional and postcolonial political tension on Fiji.

2. e.g, John D. Legge, *Britain in the Pacific Islands* (Oxford: Clarendon Press, 1960) and W. P. Morrell, *Britain in the Pacific Islands* (Oxford: Clarendon Press, 1960). For interpretations of the nature of Fijian traditions and their uses in the colonial order, see Peter France, *The Charter of the Land: Custom and Colonization in Fiji* (Melbourne: Oxford Univ. Press, 1969); Nicholas Thomas, "Material Culture and Colonial Power: Ethnological Collecting and the Establishment of Colonial Rule in Fiji," *Man*, 24,1 (Mar., 1989), 41–56 and "Sanitation and Seeing: the Creation of State Power in Early Colonial Fiji," *Comparative Studies in Society and History*, 32, I (Jan. 1990) 149–170; John Clammer, "Colonialism and Perception of Tradition in Fiji" in *Anthropology and the Colonial Encounter* (New Jersey: Humanities Press, 1973), 199–220; Margaret Jolly, "Custom and the Way of the Land: Past and Present in Vanuatu and Fiji," *Oceania*, 62 (1992) 330–354; and, especially, Martha Kaplan, *Neither Cargo Nor Cult: Ritual Politics and the Colonial Imagination in Fiji* (Durham, NC: Duke Univ. Press, 1995).

3. An edible sea slug which, like sandalwood, had considerable commercial value for the China trade.

4. Charles Wilkes, USN, *Narrative of the United States Exploring Expedition*, Vol. 111 (Philadelphia: Lea and Blanchard, 1845), 221.

5. Beche-de-mer was particularly labor intensive as it had to be cured and dried as well as collected. Cutting and hauling wood for smokehouses, stoking curing fires, and filling and loading casks required considerable local manpower. See Caroline Ralston, *Grass Huts and Warehouses: Pacific Beach Communities of the Nineteenth Century* (Honolulu: Univ. Press of Hawaii, 1978).

6. *Life in Feejee or Five Years Among the Cannibals by a Lady* (Mrs. Mary Wallis) (Ridgewood, NJ: Gregg Press, 1961. First published 1851), 250.

7. Wilkes, 182.

8. "Notes on the Background and History of the Cakobau Government," *Preliminary Inventory: Records of the Cakobau Government and the Ad-Interim Government and the Provisional Government*. Central Archives of Fiji and the Western High Commission, 1960. Copy in the Gratten Collection, Harry Ransom Humanities Research Center, University of Texas at Austin.

9. John Elphinstone Erskine, RN, *Journal of a Cruise Among the Islands of the Western Pacific* (London: John Murray, 1853), 197.

10. Thomas Williams and James Calvert, *Fiji and the Fijians* (New York: D. Appleton, 1859), 41–42.

11. Journal of Rev. W. Cross, 29 May 1841, in Deryck Scarr, "Cakobau and Ma'afu: Contenders for Preeminence in Fiji," *Pacific Islands Portraits* (Canberra: Australian National Univ. Press, 1970), 121.

12. Scarr, *Pacific Islands Portraits*, 99.

13. Williams, 2.

14. The present debate on the nature of cannibalism stems in large part from William Arens's contention the eyewitness accounts and other documen-

tation of the practice are unreliable, and the practice itself is a cultural hoax of European manufacture. [William Arens, *The Man-Eating Myth: Anthropology and Anthropophagy* (New York: Oxford Univ. Press, 1979)]. It is an argument that has found supporters among both literary scholars and cultural anthropologists. Those persuaded of cannibalism's reality as a widespread historical practice in the human community divide in turn roughly into those concerned with establishing the most basic origins of the practice (e.g., M. D. Dornstreich and G. E. B. Morren, "Does New Guinea Cannibalism Have Nutritional Value?" *Human Ecology* 2 (1974) and Michael Harner, "The Ecological Basis for Aztec Sacrifice," *American Ethnologist* 4 (1977) on the relationship between cannibalism and nutrition. For cannibalism and aggression, see Eli Sagan, *Cannibalism: Human Aggression and Cultural Form* (New York: Harper and Row, 1974) and those interested in its function and place in particular cultural constructions. Useful overviews of the issues in the debate can be found in *The Ethnography of Cannibalism*, Paula Brown and Donald Tuzin, eds. (Washington: Society for Psychological Anthropology, 1983) and "Does Man Eat Man: Inside the Great Cannibal Controversy," Lawrence Osborne, *Lingua Franca*, (April/May 1997). Of particular interest for the place of cannibalism, in particular Oceanic cultural constructs, are Ross Bowden's "Maori Cannibalism: An Interpretation," (*Oceania*, 55, 2, 1984) and Marshall Shalin's essay in *The Ethnography of Cannibalism*, "Raw Women, Cooked Men and other 'Great Things' of the Fiji Islands."

15. Wilkes recorded only one case of evidence of cannibalism observed by members of the expedition. A Fijian in a canoe pulled alongside one of the ships of the squadron, displayed a human head and then ate the eye (Wilkes, 234). Wilkes's informants on cannibalism included the Wesleyan missionary, William Hunt, who furnished an account of a cannibal feast he witnessed in February 1840 and David Whippy, an American resident in Fiji since 1825.

16. Wilkes, 96–102.

17. Wilkes, 363.

18. Wilkes, 263.

19. Wilkes, 311.

20. *Life In Feejee or Five Years Among the Cannibals by a Lady* (Mrs. Mary Wallis) (Ridgewood, NJ: Gregg Press, 1967. First Published 1851), 67, 85, 290.

21. See G. C. Henderson, *Fiji and the Fijians, 1835–1850* (Sydney: Angus and Robertson Ltd, 1931) and Basil Thomson, *The Fijians: A Study of the Decay of Custom* (London: William Heineman, 1908).

22. Williams, 161.

23. Rev. M. Russell, *Polynesia: A History of the South Sea Islands Including New Zealand* (London: T. Nelson and Sons, 1853), 265–266.

24. Erskine, 261–270.

25. Williams, 551.

26. *Life in Feejee*, iv–viii.

27. Erskine, 276.

28. Williams, 46–52.

29. Williams, 420.

30. *Life in Feejee*, 322–323.

31. Erskine, 183.

32. Erskine, 273.

33. W. P. Morrell, *Britain in the Pacific Islands* (Oxford: Clarendon Press, 1960), 131–132.

34. The U.S. consul, John Williams, most likely accidentally set fire to his own house while celebrating Independence Day with fireworks. He nonetheless held Cakobau responsible as king of Fiji and called in the power of the U.S. Navy to make a judgment (and a very favorable award) in the case. Cakobau did not retire this debt until 1869 when he made it part of his negotiations with a land company seeking holdings in Fiji.

35. "First Offer of the Cession of the Fiji Islands to the British Crown, October 12, 1858" printed in *The Evolution of Government in Fiji: A Selection of Documents and Extracts from Documents*, G. C. Henderson, ed. (Sydney: Angus and Robertson, 1935), 2–4.

36. Mrs. Smythe, *Ten Months in the Fiji Islands* (London: Hohm Henry and James Parker, 1864), ii.

37. "Instruction to Colonel Smythe from the Duke of Newcastle," appended to Smythe, 191–196.

38. Smythe, 209.

39. Smythe, 201–207.

40. A more positive view of Pritchard's efforts and a reappraisal of Smythe's role in his downfall has recently been put forward by Andres F. Robson, "The Trial of Consul Pritchard," *The Journal of Pacific History* 30, No. 2, (1995):173–193.

41. Mrs. Smythe, who accompanied her husband on his mission, for example, doubted cannibalism was in abeyance outside the Fijian Christian community. That community in 1860 was only about a third of the population. Smythe, 96.

42. Kerry Howe, *Where the Waves Fall: A History of the Pacific* (Honolulu: Univ. of Hawaii Press, 1984), 15–17.

43. For descriptions of the social and political structure of Polynesian society see Felix M. Keesing *Social Anthropology in Polynesia: A Review of Research* (London: Oxford Univ. Press, 1953); Irving Goldman, *Ancient Polynesian Society* (Chicago: Univ. of Chicago Press, 1970) and Marshall Sahlins, *Social Stratification in Polynesia* (Seattle: Univ. of Washington Press, 1958). Also Patrick V. Kirch, *The Evolution of the Polynesian Chiefdoms* (Cambridge: Cambridge Univ. Press, 1984). For Fiji, "The Stranger-King" in *Sahlins' Island of History* (Chicago: Univ. of Chicago Press, 1985) is particularly useful for its analysis of the evolution of chiefdom. Interesting arguments concerning the place of the chief in tribal society in terms of its theoretical origins and development can be found in Eli Sagan's *The Origin of Individualism, Political Oppression and the State* (New York: Knopf, 1985) and Mary W. Helms's *Craft and the Kingly Ideal: Art, Trade and Power* (Austin: Univ. of Texas Press, 1993). For the nature of chiefdom in the Pacific see Nicholas Thomas, "Marginal Powers: Shamanism and Hierarchy in Eastern Oceania" in *Shamanism, History, and the State*, Nicholas Thomas and Caroline Humphrey, eds. (Ann Arbor: Univ. of Michigan Press, 1994). Thomas's *Out of time: History and Evolution in Anthropological Discourse* (Cambridge: Cambridge Univ. Press, 1989) contains an important treatment of the cultural factors that influenced western anthropological "construction" of Polynesian/Melanesian social and political models.

44. Peter France, *Charter of the Land: Custom and Colonization in Fiji* (Melbourne: Oxford Univ. Press, 1969), 73–80.

45. J. D. Legge, *Britain in the Pacific*, 1858–1880 (London: Macmillian, 1958).

46. John Young, *Adventurous Spirits: Australian migrant society in pre-cession Fiji* (St. Lucia: Univ. of Queensland Press, 1984), 21.

47. The supply of sandalwood was exhausted everywhere in the Pacific islands by mid-century. The decline in the beche-de-mer trade had more to do with the disruptions in its principal market resulting from the Taiping Rebellion in China.

48. The number of European residents went from between four and five hundred in 1868 to at least 2000 by 1871. Frederick J. Moss, *Through Atolls and Islands in the Great South Sea* (London: Sampson Low, Marston, Searle and Rivington, 1889), 507.

49. A. L. Forbes, *Two Years in Fiji* (London: Longman's, 1857), in Young, *Adventurous Spirits*, 14.

50. Mark Francis, *Governors and Settlers: Images of Authority in the British Colonies, 1820–60* (London: Macmillan Academic and Professional Ltd, 1992), 1.

51. Edward Smith, *Fiji Times*, 1871 in Young, 25.

52. Young, 307–309.

53. Scarr, *Pacific Islands Portraits*, 117–126.

54. Cakobau basically turned the spoils of war into government financing by mortgaging lands seized from his enemies to land-hungry settlers and "leasing" prisoners of war to planters as plantation labor for £3 a head.

55. Hansard, 3rd Series, CCIX, Feb. 12, 1872, 209.

56. Letter from John Bates Thurston to Captain C. W. Hope, Dec. 6, 1873, in Deryck Scarr. "John Bates Thurston, Commodore J. G. Goodenough and Rampant Anglo-Saxons in Fiji." *Historical Studies Australia and New Zealand*, Vol. I, no. 43, 363.

57. *Fiji Times*, 4 July 1873 in Scarr, "John Bates Thurston . . . " 269.

58. Thurston Journal, 3 March 1874 in Scarr, *Pacific islands Portraits*," 121.

59. Tensions over ownership and land titles seem to have centered particularly on differing concepts of usufruct. Fijians understood ownership in terms of the right to control land use, and this right, essentially, was what they transferred to Europeans. But European concepts of land use and those of Fijians were fundamentally different. European land use concepts that included removing cultivators from land sold, commercial agriculture or speculation to the exclusion of traditional activities, and barring Fijians from any contact with alienated land if its owners so chose were alien to Fijian practice and generated considerable tension. Peter France, *The Charter of the Land*, 3–55.

60. While there is no comprehensive work on contract labor in the Pacific, there are useful studies on both the use of Pacific Islander labor and the slightly later development of Indian contract labor. For Pacific Islander labor, see, e.g., Peter Corris, *Passage, Port and Plantation: a History, of Solomon Island Labour Migration* (Canberra: Australian National Univ. Press, 1973); H. E. Maude, *Slaves in Paradise: the Peruvian Labour Trade in Polynesia, 1862–1864* (Canberra: Australian National Univ. Press, 1981): Kay Saunders, *Workers in Bondage: the Origins and Bases of Unfree Labour in Queensland, 1824–1916* (St. Lucia: Univ. of Queensland Press, 1982): *Journal of Pacific History*, 1 and 2, 1976 (special issue—the Pacific Islands Labour Trade). For

issues in Indian contract labor, see K. L. Gillion, *Fiji's Indian Migrants: a History, to the End of Indenture in 1920* (St.: Queensland Univ. Press, 1973) and Hugh Tinker, *A New System of Slavery: The Export of Indian Labour Overseas 1830–1920* (London: Hansib, 1974). Also see Kay Saunders, ed., *Indentured Labour in the British Empire, 1834–1920* (London: Croom Helm, 1984) for further background on the major issues of contract labor and migration.

61. J. D. Legge, *Britain in the Pacific, 1858–1880* (London: Macmillan, 1958), 115.

62. See Hansard, 3rd series, CCIX, c.522; CCX, c.1665–1674; CCXI, c. 184–189 for the debate on the Pacific Islanders' Protection Bill.

63. *Dictionary of National Biography*, XXII (Oxford: Oxford Univ. Press, 1938), 404.

64. Hansard, 3rd Series, CCXII, c. 192–197; CCXVI, c. 934–959; CCXXI, c. 1264–1274.

65. Hansard, House of Lords, 3rd series, vol. CCXXI, cols.81

66. Basil Thomson, *The Fijians: A Study of the Decay of Custom* (London: William Heineman, 1908), 65.

# 2
# JAPAN AND BRITISH IMPERIALISM IN AFRICA, 1870s–1930s

## Richard Bradshaw

Between the Meiji Restoration and the Second World War Japanese perceptions of British imperialism in Africa often had a profound impact on Japan. Matters of such critical importance to Japan as treaty revision, fiscal policy, imperial strategy, and commercial expansion were influenced to a far greater extent than is usually realized by Japanese reactions to British imperialism in Africa.[1]

Western historians of Anglo-Japanese relations during this period have focused on Asia, and on China in particular, as the critical region where British and Japanese interests coincided or collided. The overall importance of commercial rivalry is not often emphasized or is greatly understated in these studies.[2]

The nature of Japan's reaction to British imperialism in Africa shifted in accordance with the state of Japan's relations with Britain. Initially, during the early, vulnerable Meiji era (1870s–1880s) Japan was motivated to a large extent by a desire to revise her "unequal treaties" and to avoid falling victim to imperialism. However, during the late Meiji and early Taisho eras (1890s–1910s), Japan began to expand her empire and concluded an alliance with the British. The Japanese showed great admiration for the British Empire during this period and increased their trade with British Africa. During the early Showa period (1920s–1930s), the rapid growth of Japan's exports to Africa and British tariffs erected against them were major factors in Japan's loss of faith in Britain and her decision to abandon "free-trade" internationalism for yen-bloc autonomy.

During the first decades after the Meiji Restoration, Japanese leaders paid close attention to Britain's relationship with Egypt. In 1876 the British editor of the *Japan Weekly Mail* wrote that "no one who has watched the recent history of Japan can fail to see that it presents many points of resemblance to that of Egypt."[3] The efforts of Egyptian Khedive Ismail to promote the westernization of his country (1863–1879) began five years before the Meiji Restoration (1868). Since Japan's Meiji leaders embarked on a similar policy, they watched Egyptian affairs very closely.

When Egypt proposed the replacement of European-dominated consular courts by a system of mixed courts with both foreign and Egyptian judges in 1869,[4] the Japanese took an immediate interest because one of their first priorities was revision of their humiliating treaties with western powers. One provision of these treaties was the right of foreigners residing in Japan, when charged with breaking the law, to be tried by their own consular courts instead of by Japanese courts.[5] Egypt's proposal to set up mixed courts was a compromise which some Japanese leaders were willing to consider until the British would agree to full treaty revision.

In 1873 the Japanese sent an investigator to Egypt to study the proposed court system. After these courts began to operate, Japanese bureaucrats were assigned to write reports on how they functioned.[6] Over the next decades, until Britain agreed to treaty revision in 1894, the pros and cons of the new system were vigorously debated in Japan.[7] Numerous proposals for treaty revision advanced by the Japanese during their repeated negotiations with the British included provisions for mixed courts.[8] Japan's efforts to revise its treaties were thus clearly influenced by the Meiji leaders' study of Anglo-Egyptian relations.

During these same decades (1870s–1880s), Egypt's debt crisis and occupation by Britain had a profound impact on the Japanese. The Meiji leaders had arranged for two small loans in 1870 and 1873,[9] but they were very reluctant to borrow any more money from the west. An intense debate over this issue was provoked by a financial crisis in Japan which emerged at the same time as Egypt's debt crisis in the late 1870s.[10] The British proposed a third loan in 1879 to help the Japanese overcome their fiscal crisis. Opponents of this loan focused so often on the similarity between the debt crisis in Egypt and Japan that when the governor of Hong Kong visited Japan in 1879 and addressed the Tokyo Chamber of Commerce, he made a point of stressing the differences between Japan and Egypt in order to convince the Japanese that they did not have to be concerned about borrowing money from abroad.[11] But Egypt's demise continued to be cited by party politicians and journalists as a forewarning of what might happen if Japan borrowed foreign capital.[12] When the British eventually occupied Egypt, the Japanese naturally became all the more determined not to follow in Egypt's footsteps.

Many Japanese officials during this period, including Mori Arinori, Japan's ambassador in London between 1879 and 1884, watched closely as Egypt's debt crisis led eventually to British occupation. Mori's biographer describes the ambassador's

> haunting nightmare of Egypt—spiralling foreign debts, financial disarray, rebellion, massacre of Europeans, a foreign occupation, loss of independence—all of which transpired while Mori was accredited to the government which conducted that occupation.[13]

By the time Britain occupied Egypt in 1884, Japan's financial situation had improved considerably, and the *Japan Weekly Mail* confidently predicted that the Japanese were about to overcome their fear of incurring foreign debt. It opined that

> Japan is rapidly recovering from her unworthy and wholly erroneous apprehension that the result of pecuniary obligations incurred abroad might resemble the mishaps of Turkey or Egypt.[14]

However, this prediction was far too optimistic. A decade would pass before the Japanese would contract a foreign loan. The main reason for Japan's decision not to borrow capital from abroad, as a Finance Ministry official explained in 1897, was the danger of overdependence on foreign capital as demonstrated by Egypt and Turkey.[15] Egypt's predicament thus served as a cautionary tale for the Japanese, discouraging any dependence on foreign capital for their program of modernization.

But if Egypt's debt crisis and occupation by Britain was a warning for many Japanese, for others it suggested how Japan might extend its own imperial influence. Soon after the outbreak of the Sino-Japanese War in October 1894, former foreign minister Inoue Kaoru was sent to Korea as Japan's "Extraordinary Envoy." Shortly after his arrival, he wrote to Japanese Prime Minister Itô Hirobumi that he thought Japan should pursue the same policy in Korea "which England follows in Egypt."[16] Inoue subsequently explained this idea with a great deal of candor.

> What was England's pretext for intervening in Egypt? Was it not the fact that England had obtained a position of real interest there by supplying Egypt with capital? I firmly believe that if we wish to solidify our position in Korea and establish a pretext for intervention in its internal affairs, we

> must obtain real interests there, whether through railroads or through loans, and by financial means create pretexts for extending our intervention to other kinds of relationships.[17]

Inoue was a bureaucrat with close ties to Japanese business circles. It is not surprising that he thought British bureaucrats and bankers had worked closely together to create a justification for Britain's intervention in Egypt. However, Inoue exaggerated the degree of collaboration between British bureaucrats and bankers with regard to Egypt and overestimated the degree of influence that he had with Japanese bankers, who in fact proved unwilling to extend the huge loans he urged. As Peter Duus remarks, "Big capital was less prepared for the 'Egyptianization' of Korea than Inoue was."[18] Inoue's schemes to turn Korea into an "Egyptian-type" protectorate failed. In May 1895, the American, German, British, and Russian ministers communicated their strong disapproval of Japan's attempts to secure special concessions in Korea.

The intervention of western powers in Korea to block Inoue's designs combined with the Triple Intervention by Russia, Germany, and France in 1895 to make it clear to Japanese officials that Japan needed a strong ally. This was one of the factors that encouraged a number of Japanese officials to begin promoting the idea of an alliance between Japan and Britain. A number of newspapers that generally supported the government, including the *Jiji Shimpo* and the *Nichi Nichi*, began to argue the merits of a pro-British alliance.[19]

Britain pursued a policy of "splendid isolation"[20] at this time and thus was not eager to ally itself with any power, but the Anglo-Boer War in South Africa at the turn of the century (1899–1902) made Britain feel more vulnerable. By both draining Britain financially and drawing her attention to the need for a strong ally in the East, the Anglo-Boer War helped set the stage for the formation of the Anglo-Japanese Alliance immediately after the conflict.[21]

During Britain's initial reverses in the war, the Japanese press refrained from passing judgment on the war, but by the end of December 1899, the press began to express its views.[22] Then, as the British managed to overcome their Boer adversaries in spite of widespread hostility to Britain in Europe, many Japanese elites were impressed. The *Nichi Nichi* acknowledged that there were those in Japan happy to see the British suffer reverses in South Africa because Britain was, in their eyes, "a species of all-consuming monster."[23] But these critics were wrong, it explained, because Britain was, in fact, Japan's friend.

The *Jimmin* pointed out the many advantages to be gained by British victory which would put a stop to Boer racial prejudice and introduce the "the best type of civilization" into South Africa.[24] Even the *Nippon*, known for its opposition to excessive westernization, had generous praise for the British. Japan, the *Nippon* explained, had begun to look to Britain as her primary source of support and even as a potential ally.[25]

Meanwhile, noted Japanophile Arthur Doísy told a British audience that the Japanese rejoiced "in our victories and sorrowed at our losses almost as much as we did in England."[26] Doísy informed another audience that a Japanese gentleman in Ontario had urged

> that Great Britain should accept the services of sufficient Japanese troops to bring the war in South Africa to a speedy end. When this . . . had been achieved, . . . British troops would be free to meet Russia's next move against India.[27]

The attitude of most Japanese differed from that of many Europeans at this time, particularly Germans. The strain put on Anglo-German relations by the war and the boost it gave to Anglo-Japanese relations were factors that paved the way for the Anglo-Japanese Alliance in 1902. The main point of common interest, though, was a desire to check the Russians. Katsura Tarô, Japan's prime minister, during a critical period in the negotiations leading up to the alliance, later recalled that

> there was no scope for Britain to extend its power in the Far East because of the [South] African war . . . [and] Russia, taking advantage of British preoccupations, was using it as an opportunity to expand its own power there. This was certainly the reason for Britain's approach to us.[28]

On the Japanese side, not only was there hope that the alliance would help Japan achieve its goals in East Asia but also that it would allow Japanese commercial expansion throughout the world. Foreign Minister Komura Jutarô argued in December 1901 for cooperation with Britain on the grounds that Britain had colonies on "five continents." The benefits that Japan would gain from emigration and trade in these colonies, he argued, would far exceed those to be derived from Manchuria and Siberia.[29]

In fact, Japan's alliance with Britain in 1902 facilitated both increased trade in world markets and the development of its imperial influence in East Asia by keeping other great powers from interfering during the Russo-Japanese War. Soon after war broke out in 1904, the Japanese forced a treaty upon the Koreans that turned their country into a virtual protectorate of Japan.[30]

The conclusion of the Anglo-Japanese Alliance and Japan's growing influence in Korea further stimulated Japanese interest in British colonial administration in Egypt. Japanese officials expressed their desire to obtain copies of Lord Cromer's report on Egypt.[31] Simultaneously, British diplomats showed themselves favorably disposed toward Japan's role in Korea,[32] comparing Japan's position there with Britain's imperial presence in Egypt. In March 1904 the British minister in Seoul, John Newall Jordan, reported that in his opinion Japan would undoubtedly "succeed in Egyptianising Korea . . . "[33]

Japan's study of British rule in Egypt was evident in the program of "reform" which the Japanese presented to the Korean government in August of 1904. Jordan commented that the Japanese

> appear to have followed with some closeness the model set by Britain in Egypt and to have given concrete expression at the outset to the functions which, as gradually defined, were exercised by the early British Financial adviser in [Egypt].[34]

A series of books on British administration in Egypt was subsequently published in Japanese over the next few years.[35] This not only reflected the desire of the Japanese to know more about how to rule their nascent empire but also how to justify their colonial rule in terms acceptable to their ally.

The official Japanese attitude toward British imperialism in Africa was most positive in the period between the Boer War and the First World War. During the First World War, however, signs of strain in Anglo-Japanese relations surfaced in various ways. Japan's more aggressive policy toward China was the main point of dispute, but the dramatic increase in Japan's exports during the war to markets as distant as British colonies in Africa indicated what would soon emerge as a major source of tension in Anglo-Japanese relations: growth of Japanese trade coincident with decline of Britain's textile industry.

## TRADE RIVALRY AND ITS IMPACT ON ANGLO-JAPANESE RELATIONS

Between 1913 and 1938, British exports of cotton cloth decreased by 80 percent[36] while Japanese exports of cotton fabrics increased 1,000 percent.[37] African markets never took a large share of Japan's total exports of cotton goods,[38] but the freedom of Japanese goods to move into new African markets during the early 1930s, particularly in the face of Chinese boycotts,[39] became a decisive factor in determining whether Japan's exports of cotton goods would continue to grow or begin to decline. When barriers were raised against Japan's exports to Africa in the 1930s, Britain and her allies were held largely to blame for the subsequent decline in the fortunes of Japan's leading industry.

The value of Japan's exports to Africa rose from around 44 million yen in 1928 to around 243 million in 1937, an increase of over 500 percent.[40] In the critical period between 1930 and 1934 the quantity of British cotton piece goods exported to Africa decreased by 20 percent, while Japanese cotton piece goods increased by 264 percent.[41] By 1933 Japan had surpassed Britain as the world's leading exporter of cotton piece goods, African markets providing an important new destination for the continuing growth of Japan's textile industry. But, between 1933 and 1935, trade barriers limited Japan's expansion into these key markets in Africa.[42] Having reached its peak of over 2.7 billion square yards in 1935, Japan's total exports of cotton goods fell steadily thereafter. Fifty years of growth in Japan's leading industry had come to an end.

The greatest disappointment for Japan was the reversal of its fortunes in trade with Egypt. After rising from 46.1 million to 141.1 million square yards between 1930 and 1935, Japan's exports of cotton goods to Egypt decreased dramatically after 1935 to a mere 10.4 million square meters in 1938.[43] Subsequently, the Japanese were almost completely shut out of this market.[44]

The Egyptians started to restrict Japanese imports as soon as they gained tariff autonomy in 1930. But Japan, in order to protect her own fledgling textile industry, continued to pour cotton goods into Egypt and displace British exports during the early 1930s. Between 1931 and 1935 Egypt's cotton imports from Britain fell by two-thirds (from 92 to 30 million square meters).[45] It was not only British textiles which felt the pressure. Japan had begun to provide more semi-processed inputs for Egyptian industries and a wide variety of other goods that competed with British imports.[46]

The British took advantage of their position as the largest purchaser of Egyptian cotton to pressure Egypt into giving preference to British goods. In July 1935, the Egyptian government formally renounced the Egyptian-Japanese Commercial Treaty (1930), giving Japan only three months' notice. Then, in September 1935, Egypt imposed a depreciated-currency surtax of 40 percent on all Japanese cotton and rayon goods. The Japanese responded by sending a delegation to Egypt which attempted to negotiate a new commercial treaty and to modify the measures that had been taken against Japanese trade. But by November the efforts of these Japanese representative had failed.[48]

Egyptian trade restrictions on Japanese goods were not aimed at helping the British. Although imports of British goods increased in 1936, they fell thereafter as Egyptian goods began to displace them. Nevertheless, the Japanese detected the hand of the British behind the scenes. The British high commissioner in Egypt at this time, Sir Miles Lampson, had formerly served in China, where he had incurred the wrath of the Japanese because of his pro-Chinese stance.[49]

Japanese exports to the Union of South Africa[50] also came under severe attack in the early 1930s. These attacks were often linked to white South African fears of a "Yellow Peril,"[51] which confirmed Japanese suspicions that discrimination against their exports was related to anti-Asian racism. In fact, the two issues were soon connected in South Africa. The first outbreak of anti-Japanese sentiment in South Africa occurred in the spring of 1931 when the public learned that its government had concluded a gentleman's agreement with Japan in October of 1930 that removed legal restrictions on Japanese residence and movement in the Cape and Natal. This agreement, which is the origin of "honorary white" status for Japanese in South Africa, was concluded in order to facilitate Japanese purchase of South African wool.[52]

In response to demands to protect South African industry,[53] the government imposed new duties on imports and passed an anti-currency depreciation tariff in 1932 that was essentially aimed at the Japanese. Imports from Japan dropped slightly in 1932, but then began to rise dramatically again in 1933, leading to another outburst of anti-Japanese rhetoric. The Japanese responded by promising to renew their efforts to increase purchases of South African wool.[54] Japan's purchase of wool did not show any signs of a significant increase, however, except in 1937. As a report by a Japanese business organization in that year indicated,

> every newspaper [in South Africa] has been running articles on Japanese insincerity and on the unfair competition of Japanese traders. Anti-Japanese sentiment is increasing dramatically as the mood of the people grows more hostile to Japan and its products.[55]

The fears of some South African whites were exacerbated by their concern that the Japanese might start colonizing Africa and that some South African blacks were beginning to believe that the Japanese might help liberate them. There were rumors of possible Japanese settlement in Portuguese Africa and in West Africa, and talk of

Ethiopian concessions to the Japanese.[56] Such rumors, together with South African fears that the Japanese posed a potential military threat to their country, fed anti-Japanese sentiment in South Africa.[57] Racism played a central role in the hostility expressed by many white South Africans who welcomed further white settlement in Africa but feared Japanese settlement. The Japanese knew that such racism was prevalent among the British as well as the Afrikaners.

As Japan's exports to its "old markets" were restricted by boycotts, bigotry, and trade barriers, the Japanese increasingly placed their hopes in the possibility of "new markets"[58] in East and West Africa.[59] They were very successful in East Africa because a number of overlapping treaties made it difficult for the British to restrict Japan's trade in their East African empire.[60] This very success, however, demonstrated to the Japanese what would have been possible if restrictions had not been placed on their trade elsewhere.

In West Africa, Japan's access to local markets was assured by the Anglo-Japanese Commercial Treaty of 1911, but when Japan's exports to West Africa expanded rapidly in the early 1930s, the British responded by imposing tariffs against Japanese goods in Sierra Leone and Gambia in 1932. In the spring of 1933, while the British and the Japanese were engaged in negotiations regarding commercial conflicts, the secretary of state for the colonies asked all colonial governments to refrain from further restrictions on Japanese goods because the British government wanted to "avoid anything indicating a concerted 'drive' against Japanese imports into the British Empire" as the "cumulative effect" of such measures might harm Britain's "cordial relations" with Japan.[61]

After negotiations proved unsuccessful, further limits to Japanese imports into British West Africa were implemented that seemed to be very effective. In the case of Sierra Leone, for example, imports of Japanese cotton piece goods fell from 911,418 square yards in the first half of 1934 to only 29,186 square yards during the second half of that year.[62]

## JAPANESE RESENTMENT

Studies of Anglo-Japanese relations during the 1930s by non-Japanese scholars tend to focus on conflicts of interest in East Asia. In contrast, Japanese authors of both the prewar and postwar generations have often put greater emphasis on trade rivalry. In 1935, for example, Ishimaru Tôta published a book entitled *Japan Must Fight Britain* in which he wrote:[63]

> The British Colonies and Dependencies were not justified in thus raising tariff walls. Japanese goods had . . . spread over Kenya, Uganda, Tanganyika and Egypt, where they had captured the markets and driven out British goods. Japan had beaten Britain by two to one in Egypt and by four to one in East Africa . . . it was only in South and West Africa that British goods predominated.

In the late 1930s Japanese diplomats often tried to impress upon their western counterparts the importance of finding markets for Japanese trade. When recently appointed Japanese ambassador to Britain Yoshida Shigeru called on American Ambassador Grew in April of 1936, he complained that

> foreign countries should realize the seriousness of [Japan's] situation and endeavor to help Japan . . . that it was principally a matter of finding outlets for Japan's trade. . . . the hardships of the world depression had been compounded by restrictive tariffs against Japanese exports, particularly textiles . . .[64]

A Japanese commentator writing in the influential *Gaikô Jihô* [*Journal of Foreign Relations*] in the late 1930s explained that "the Japanese are having markets closed to them . . . Inevitably they seek to maintain a life-line in neighboring China . . ."[65] During a debate in 1938 between the Japanese editor of the *Tôyô Keizai Shinpô* [*Oriental Economic Review*] and a British correspondent for *The Times* the former explained that the Japanese were upset by the degree to which British possessions around the world had been closed to Japan's peaceful economic expansion.[66]

Japan's exports to Africa increased dramatically throughout Africa in the 1930s, and Britain's attempts to restrict these exports to African markets contributed to Japan's loss of faith in the possibility of cooperation with Britain.

## CONCLUSION

From the Meiji Restoration until the Second World War, British colonialism in Africa often had a dramatic impact on Japan. The Meiji Restoration coincided with the European Partition of Africa, and the rapid growth of British colonialism served as a warning for the Japanese, who were determined to avoid the fate of African states such as Egypt by not becoming dependent on foreign capital.

By the late Meiji era Japan had so successfully transformed itself that it was able to embark on a policy of colonial expansion, at which point Japan's leaders studied British colonialism in Africa in order to develop her own colonial administration along British lines and to justify her colonial rule by using the same language as the British. Thus British colonialism in Africa, particularly in Egypt, served as a model for Japanese colonialism.

Between the late Meiji era and the Second World War, Japanese leaders turned their attention to British colonial markets in Africa as Japan's exports of cheap textiles to these markets grew, particularly during the 1930s. Access to these markets became a matter of increasing importance to Japan when the Chinese boycotted Japanese goods in protest against Japanese economic and political imperialism. British efforts to limit Japan's access to colonial markets in Africa was an important and usually overlooked factor in Japan's growing determination to preserve for itself a special sphere of influence in Asia.

Japanese reactions to formal and informal British imperialism in Asia have been well studied, but the degree to which Japanese leaders, and perhaps other Asian leaders as well, were influenced by their perception of British colonialism in Africa is a promising new topic just beginning to be explored.

## REFERENCES

1. See Richard Bradshaw, "Japan and European Colonialism in Africa, 1800–1937," Ph.D. diss., Ohio Univ., March 1992; Morikawa Jun, *Minami Afurika to Nihon* [*South Africa and Japan*] (Tokyo: Dobunkan, 1988); Okakura Takashi and Kitagawa Katsuhiko, *Nihon Afurika Koryushi* [*A History of African-Japanese Relations*] (Tokyo: Dobunkan, 1993).

2. Ian Nish, for example, suggests that "commercial factors were probably of minor importance when it came to policy-making: but it did affect the atmosphere in which the Japanese problem was debated in Britain." ("Japan in Britain's View of the International System, 1919–37," in Ian Nish, ed., *Anglo-Japanese Alienation: Papers of the Anglo-Japanese Conference on the History of the Second World War* [Cambridge: Cambridge Univ. Press, 1979], 53).

3. *Japan Weekly Mail* (henceforth *JWM*), 27 May 1876, 463.

4. John Marlowe, *A History of Modern Egypt and Anglo-Egyptian Relations, 1800–1953* (New York: Shoestring Press, 1954), 83.

5. See F. C. Jones, *Extraterritoriality in Japan and the Diplomatic Relations Resulting in its Abolition, 1853–1899* (New Haven: AMS Press, 1931).

6. Fukuchi Genichirô, "Gaikokujin Tachiai Saiban Hôkoku" [*A Report on Foreign Courts of Justice*] (1873); J. R. Davidson, "Ejiputo Kyôritsu Saiban Hôkoku Sho [*Report on Egypt's Mixed Courts*] (1877); and Mitsukuri Rinshô, "Ejiputo Hôritsu Sho" [*Report on Egypt's Legal System*] (1878). Discussion of these reports can be found in Inô Tetsutarô, *Gaibun Shisô Ronkô* [*An Essay on Foreign Policy Thought*] (Tokyo, 1966), vol. 1, 233–234; James Huffman, *Politics of the Meiji Press: The Life of Fukuchi Gen'ichiro* (Honolulu,

1980), 71–2; Furukawa, "Nihon Afurika Kôshô Shi," 50; Albert Altman, "The Emergence of the Press in Meiji Japan," Ph.D. diss., Princeton Univ., 1965, 134.

7. For sample editorials on mixed courts see *Tokyo Nichi Nichi*, 5–7 Feb. 1876, and their translations in the *JWM*, 12 February 1876, 146–48. On a party politician's objections to the adoption of Egyptian-style mixed courts, see Sandra T. W. Davis, "Treaty Revision, National Security, and Regional Co-operation: A *Mintoo* Viewpoint," in Hilary Conroy, Sandra Davis and Wayne Patterson, eds., *Japan in Transition: Thought and Action in the Meiji Era, 1868–1912* (Madison, NJ: Fairleigh Dickinson Univ. Press, 1984), 154.

8. Louis Perez, "Mutsu Munemitsu and the Revision of the 'Unequal Treaties'," Ph.D. diss., Univ. of Michigan, 1986.

9. See Grace Fox, *Britain and Japan, 1858–1883* (Oxford: Oxford Univ. Press, 1969), especially Ch. 3, "British Banks, Loans, and Bankers."

10. The cost of suppressing the Satsuma Rebellion in 1877 contributed to this financial crisis, as did the issuing of too much inconvertible paper currency.

11. See John Pope Hennessy's address to the Tokyo Chamber of Commerce in the *JWM*, 21 June 1879, 797–8.

12. See discussions of the issue in *JWM*, 27 May 1876, 463, and 4 December 1880, 1570, for example.

13. Ivan P. Hall, *Mori Arinori* (Cambridge: Cambridge Univ. Press, 1973), 286.

14. *JWM*, 28 June 1884, 608–9.

15. E. H. Norman, *Japan's Emergence as a Modern Japanese State* (1975), 222–23. William Lockwood writes that the "Japanese were wary of financial imperialism, seeing it in operation among their Asiatic neighbors" (*The Economic Development of Japan*, 253), but Jean-Pierre Lehmann notes that ". . . the Japanese were not only acutely conscious of what was happening in China in terms of spiralling foreign indebtedness, but . . . [were] more than dimly aware of comparable developments in places such as Egypt and Turkey" (*The Roots of Modern Japan* [New York: St. Martin's Press, 1982], 174).

16. Inoue to Itô, 25 December 1894, as translated in William B. Beasley, *Japanese Imperialism 1894–1945* (Oxford: Oxford Univ. Press, 1987), 51.

17. Peter Duus, *The Abacus and the Sword: The Japanese Penetration of Korea, 1895–1910* (Berkeley: Univ. of California Press, 1995), 92.

18. Duus, *The Abacus and the Sword*, 93.

19. Ian Nish, *Anglo-Japanese Alliance* (London, 1966), 367.

20. "Splendid isolation" was a term used at this time to describe Britain's lack of any military alliances which could draw it into another nation's war.

21. Shigeru Murashima, "Boa Senso To Nihon: Nichi-Ei Domei E No Ichi Dotei" [The Boer War and Japan: One Step on the Way to the Anglo-Japanese Alliance] *Gunji Shigaku* [*Journal of Military History*] 25, 1 (June 1989), 4–19.

22. *JWM*, 23 December 1899, 635.

23. See translated synopsis in *JWM*, 23 December 1899, 636.

24. See translated synopsis in *JWM*, 23 December 1899, 636.

25. See translations in *JWM*, 10 February 1900, 137, and 17 February 1900, 163.

26. *Bristol Mercury*, 6 February 1900, cited in John Adlard, *A Biography*

*of Arthur Diósy, Founder of the Japan Society: Home to Japan* (Lewiston: Edwin Mellon Press, 1990), 116.

27. *Daily Mail*, 17 January 1900, cited in Adlard, *A Biography of Arthur Diósy*, 117.

28. Nish, *The Anglo-Japanese Alliance*, 380.

29. Nish, *The Anglo-Japanese Alliance*, 383–85.

30. Wayne Patterson, "Japanese Imperialism in Korea: A Study of Immigration and Foreign Policy," in Hilary Conroy, Sandra Davis and Wayne Patterson (eds.), *Japan in Transition: Thought and Action in the Meiji Era, 1868–1912* (Madison, NJ: Fairleigh Dickinson Univ. Press, 1984), 304–305.

31. Emmanuel Ofori Adu, "British Diplomatic Attitudes towards Japanese Economic and Political Activities in Korea, South Manchuria, Kwantung and Shantung 1904–1922," Ph.D. diss., Univ. of London, 1976, 50.

32. As early as 1899, Lord Beresford had proposed that Britain and Japan co-operate in playing a role in China similar to that of Britain in Egypt (Frank G. Williston, "The End of British Isolation: The Origins of the Anglo-Japanese Alliance," Ph.D. diss., Univ. of Chicago, 1935, 93).

33. Jordan to Lansdowne (No. 8 Confidential), 16 March 1904, FO 17/1659, Public Record Office, London (henceforth PRO).

34. Jordan to Lansdowne (No. 199 Confidential), 19 October 1904, FO 17/1660, PRO.

35. Kato Fuso, *Hogokoku Keiei No Mohan Ejiputo* [Egypt: A Model for the Administration of Protectorates] (1905); Inoue Masaji, *Cho Koku Keiei Shiryô—Ejiputo Ni Okeru Eikoku [Resource Material for the Administration of Korea—The British in Egypt]* (1906); Kamata Eikichi, *Ejiputokoku No Zaisei—Taiwan Zaisei Sanko Shiryô [Egypt's Financial Affairs—Reference Materials for Taiwan's Financial Affairs]* (1909).

36. John Singleton, *Lancashire on the Scrapheap: The Cotton Industry 1945–1970* (Leeds, England: Maney Publishing, 1991).

37. Keizo Seki, *The Cotton Industry of Japan* (Tokyo: I$^{st}$ Japan Society, 1956), 307, Table 9: Japanese exports of cotton fabrics increased from 235,177,000 square yards in 1913 to a peak of 2,709,885,000 sq. yds. in 1935.

38. Africa's share of Japan's exports was about 8 percent between 1934–35 (Economic Planning Agency, *Economic Survey of Japan (1959–1960)* [Tokyo, 1960], 323).

39. China's share of Japan's exports dropped to 14 percent in 1932, largely due to boycotts (C. F. Remer, *A Study of Chinese Boycotts* [Baltimore, 1933], 235). As Roger Louis notes in *British Strategy in the Far East* (Oxford: Clarendon Press), 220, a British Foreign Office report in December 1931 on Anglo-Japanese trade relations "concluded that Japanese exports to China had declined from 1930 to 1931 by 120 million yen but that this loss had been recouped in other markets—mainly those of the British Empire."

40. Bureau of Statistics, *Japan Statistical Yearbook 1955/56* (Tokyo, 1956), 253.

41. The quantity of British cotton piece goods dropped from 402 million yards in 1930 to 320.2 million yards in 1934, while the quantity of Japanese goods rose from 177.8 million yards to 469 million yards in the same period (*Bulletin d'Informations Économiques et Financières Japonaises*, 10, 35 [June 1935], 14).

42. On 4 July 1933 the Japanese received notice that after 16 May 1934

the Anglo-Japanese commercial treaty of 1911, with reference to British protectorates, colonies and mandates in Africa, would become null and void. *OM & TNN*, 5 July 1933.

43. Shimizu Hiroshi, *Anglo-Japanese Trade Rivalry in the Middle East in the Inter-War Period* (London: Oxford Univ. Press, 1986), 99.

44. Regarding Anglo-Japanese trade rivalry in Egypt during this period see E 3.1.1/2 Kakkoku Bôeki Seisaku Kankei Zakken [*Matters Relating to the Trade Policies of Various Countries*], especially E 3.1.1/2–15 Dôjô: Ejiputokoku No Bu [*Same: Egypt*], in the Diplomatic Records Office in Tokyo, Japan; Overseas Economic Survey, *Egypt* (London, 1933); Lampson (Cairo) to Eden, "Report on Economic Situation Egypt," 16 March 1936, FO 371/20140 J 2325/606/126; and Japanese newspapers such as the *Osaka Mainichi and Tokyo Nichi Nichi* which followed events in Egypt very closely because Osaka was the main textile-producing region in Japan at this point.

45. Shimizu, *Anglo-Japanese Trade Rivalry*, 99.

46. *OM & TNN*, 9 November 1932, and Memorandum by the British Commercial Secretary in Cairo on Japanese competition affecting British goods, forwarded by High Commissioner Sir M. Lampson to the Foreign Office, 26 May 1934, FO 371/18171, PRO.

47. On the relative position of Britain and Japan as importers of Egyptian exports, see *OM & TNN*, 21 July 1935.

48. *OM & TNN*, 15 and 27 November 1935.

49. Lampson is specifically mentioned in *OM & TNN*, 8 August 1935.

50. The value of Japanese exports to the Union of South Africa rose from c. 14 million yen to 53 million yen between 1930 and 1937.

51. See Hedley A. Chilvers, *The Yellow Man Looks On: Being the Story of the Anglo-Dutch Conflict in South Africa and Its Interest for the Peoples of Asia* (London: Cassell, 1933).

52. Arguments for and against the agreement can be found in Union of South Africa, *Debates of the House of Assembly*, Vol. 17, 1931, and in newspapers such as the *Rand Daily Mail* in South African and the previously cited *OM & TNN* in Japan.

53. Six Johannesburg factories closed in 1933 as the result of "unforeseen and ruinous Japanese competition" ("The Rising Sun of Japan," *Fortune*, 1937, cited in Frank Gibney, *Japan: The Fragile Super Power* [Tokyo and Rutland, 1996], 44).

54. Commercial Counselor G. B. Sansom (Tokyo), "Japanese Trade with South Africa," enclosure in British Minister F. O. Lindley (Tokyo) to John Simon, 5 March 1934; "Trade Agreement Between Japan and the Union of South Africa," FO 371 F 21181/159/23.

55. Nihon Gomu Seihin Yushutsu Kumiai Chôsa Kenkyû [*Japan Rubber Products Export Association*], *Minami Afurika Renpô* [The Union of South Africa] (Tokyo, 1937), 3, cited in Morikawa, *Minami Afurika To Nihon*, 13 [my translation].

56. Union of South Africa, *Debates*, Vol. 22, 7 March 1934, and High Commissioner P. Lieschin to Secretary of State for Dominon Affairs J. H. Thomas, 15 March 1934, Sir H. F. Batterbee (Dominons Office) to Sir George Mounsey, 1 August 1934, C. T. Te Water (London) to J. H. Thomas, 23 May 1934; Staff Office (Cape Town Intelligence) to Director of Naval Intelligence (Admiralty), 23 May 1934, all in FO 371/18188, and Angolan Consul General

Francis O'Meara to Secretary of State for Foreign Affairs, 31 July 1934, FO 371/18173, PRO.

57. The fears of South African whites with regard to the military threat were not entirely unfounded. See Eric Rosenthal, *Japan's Bid for Africa, Including the Story of the Madagascar Campaign* (Johannesburg: Central News Agency, 1944).

58. Osamu Ishii, *Cotton-Textile Diplomacy: Japan, Great Britain and the United States, 1930–1936* (New York, 1981), 222.

59. Kweku Ampiah, "British Commercial Policies Against Japanese Expansionism in East and West Africa, 1932–1935," *The International Journal of African Historical Studies* 23, 4 (1990), 619–41.

60. Japan became a party to the Congo Basin treaties after the First World War, which guaranteed free access to many African markets, including Kenya, Uganda, Ruanda-Urundi, and Tanganyika. She also had free access to League of Nation mandates, including Ruanda-Urundi, Tanganyika, French Cameroons, British Cameroon, French Togoland, and British Togoland (Miriam S. Farley, *The Problem of Japanese Trade Expansion in the Post-War Situation.* [New York: International Secretariat, Institute of Pacific Relations, 1940], 81).

61. Caine (Colonial Office) to Randall, 29 March 1934, FO 371/18170 F 1731/159/23, PRO. Also see enclosure, "Cabinet Memorandum by the Secretary of State for the Colonies," in Farley, *The Problem of Japanese Trade Expansion*, 81.

62. Kweku Ampiah, "British Commercial Policies against Japanese Expansionism in East and West Africa, 1932–1935," *The International Journal of African Historical Studies*, 23, 4 (1990), 632.

63. Ishimaru, Tota, *Japan Must Fight Britain* (London: G. V. Raymond 1935), 82.

64. Ambassador Grew, April 30, 1936, quoted in J. W. Dower, *Empire and Aftermath: Yoshida Shigeru and the Japanese Experience, 1878–1954* (Cambridge and London: Harvard Univ. Press, 1979), 115–116.

65. Usui Katsumi, "A Consideration of Anglo-Japanese Relations: Japanese Views of Britain, 1937–41," in Ian Nish, ed., *Anglo-Japanese Alienation*, 84.

66. Katsumi, "Anglo-Japanese Relations," 87.

# 3

# CONSEQUENCES OF THE BRITISH OCCUPATION OF ETHIOPIA DURING WORLD WAR II

**Theodore M. Vestal**

The Federal Democratic Republic of Ethiopia (FDRE) is a troubled state. One of the least developed nations of the world, the FDRE came into existence under a questionable mandate on 21 August 1995 and since then has been severely criticized for abusing human rights, thwarting democratic processes, and fostering "ethnic federalism" based on ethnic distrust and hatred.[1] The dominant "Woyane" Tigrean Peoples Liberation Front (TPLF), linchpin of the ruling Ethiopian Peoples Revolutionary Democratic Front (EPRDF) coalition, epitomizes the antipathy among ethnic groups in its thinly disguised discrimination against Amharas. The eastern part of the country, where wars have been fought over territories claimed by "Greater Somalia," is bedeviled by armed conflicts between FDRE and antigovernment forces. Other opponents of the current regime criticize the government's acquiescence in "giving away" the former province of Eritrea, now an independent and sovereign nation.

Although the origins of many of the FDRE's difficulties can be traced not only to internal tensions but also to Cold War rivalries between the United States and the Soviet Union in the Horn of Africa, at least three of the major problems plaguing the fledgling republic—those concerned with Eritrea, Somalia, and the aversion of the Woyane toward the Amharas—can be attributed, at least in part, to British military occupation and administration of Ethiopia and neighboring areas from 1941–1952. This chapter will review significant events during that period when Great Britain was the hegemonic power in the Horn and attempt to relate them to the three present day problems in Ethiopia.

## BRITISH INTEREST IN THE HORN OF AFRICA

The interests of the British Empire in the Horn of Africa were strategic and economic. Strategically, control of the Horn helped to safeguard British world power. As pointed out by Robinson and Gallagher (1961), the Mediterranean and Indian interests were the driving wheel in the machine of Empire, and the Horn of Africa was one of several lesser wheels connecting them. But British territorial claims in the lands bordering the Red Sea were not made for the sake of African empire or commerce as such. They were part of a giant security system protecting communication links among the British Isles, the Mediterranean, and India.[2] Great Britain's position in the world depended upon the security of these communications until the end of World War II and the ensuing collapse of her colonial empire. After 1945, new security interests came into play with the Horn of Africa helping to hold the Soviets at bay in Africa and serving as a safeguard for the passage of the Middle Eastern oil that was becoming indispensable to Western Europe.[3]

In the late nineteenth and early twentieth centuries, the British encouraged Egyptian and especially Italian territorial ambitions in the Horn to counter French, Russian, or Belgian designs on the region. The Italians colonized Eritrea and Italian Somaliland. The French occupied the strategic port of Djibouti and surrounding lands. And the British themselves claimed a portion of Somaliland and exercised their influence in the Anglo-Egyptian Sudan.

During World War I, Great Britain's imperial ambition included a project for establishing a protectorate over Abyssinia, which was thought to offer scope for commercial concessions and white settlement. But the scheme encountered diplomatic and economic obstacles and was abandoned in 1919. Thereafter, the British were content to tolerate an uncolonized Ethiopia, so long as no enemies were in control of the Red Sea ports. Until the 1930s, the British government believed that her commercial interests would prevail in an undivided Ethiopia that would promote wider equality of commercial opportunity. Thus, Britain's informal imperialism in an unpartitioned Ethiopia probably saved Abyssinian territorial integrity.[4]

## THE BONDING OF BRITAIN AND ETHIOPIA: WORLD WAR II

The destinies of the British and the Ethiopian empires became physically entwined in 1936 when Emperor Haile Selassie, following his defeat by Mussolini's fascist army, took up residence in exile in Great Britain. Although many Britons were outraged by the "betrayal" of Ethiopia by the League of Nations in the mid-1930s, the British Government was reluctant to give the emperor recognition. Indeed, some British colonial officers had "a great deal of sympathy for the Italian settlers and administrators . . . who in the few years they had been in Abyssinia were making a titanic effort to produce another model colony."[5]

These attitudes changed when Italy declared war on Great Britain on 10 June 1940, and the British allowed the emperor to fly to the Sudan to take part in the "Liberation Campaign" to free the Italian colonies. At that time, the British Foreign Office scarcely envisioned any real restoration of Ethiopian independence. A Foreign Office memo of 9 December 1940 stated:

> It is difficult to believe that the restoration of the former Ethiopian Empire as an independent state is a practicable aim. The Empire survived as long as it did only because the three Great Powers bordering on it—Great Britain, France and Italy—were unable to agree on its control. A solution might be to aim at the restoration of the ex-Emperor as the ruler of a native African state under European protection . . . It is not necessary to decide now what European power would exercise the protectorate.[6]

Such sentiments were echoed by some British colonialists in Africa who coveted the Ethiopian highlands "where the earth was fertile and hospitable."[7] But dreams of empire were put on hold while Britain struggled to turn the tide of the war which was not going well in 1940.

The battered Allies needed a success on the battlefield to boost their spirits, and they got one in East Africa in early 1941. The Allied offensive swept the Italians out of Ethiopia and the Horn, and on 5 May 1941, Haile Selassie reentered Addis Ababa—the first victory of the Allies in World War II. Strategy and tactics of the campaign were determined almost entirely by the British, who from the outset planned to assume the dominant military role for themselves and to assign the emperor and the Ethiopians only a minor and ancillary one in geographically difficult terrain.[8]

Allied success compelled Great Britain to commit itself to a definite policy for Ethiopia much sooner than originally expected. On 4 February, Foreign Secretary Anthony Eden for the first time gave public recognition to the principle of Ethiopian independence: "His Majesty's Government would welcome the reappearance of an independent Ethiopian state and recognize the claim of the Emperor Haile

Selassie to the throne."[9] Eden affirmed that Britain would provide assistance and guidance in economic and political matters subject to international arrangement at the conclusion of the peace. The foreign secretary further avowed that Great Britain had no territorial ambitions in Abyssinia. In the meantime, he noted, the conduct of military operations by imperial forces would require temporary measures of military control. Those would be carried out in consultation with the emperor and would be brought to an end as soon as the situation permitted.

The successful Liberation Campaign came to an end a short time later. Ironically, the British, in accepting the surrender of Italian forces in Addis Ababa, were a party to the first act in the decolonization of the European empires that was to take place over the next 35 years.[10]

## BRITISH MILITARY ADMINISTRATION, 1941–1942

Despite Eden's encouraging rhetoric, infringements of Ethiopian sovereignty were soon unilaterally imposed by British military authorities. Ethiopians resented these restrictions, noting that no comparable policy was adopted in the case of European countries freed from the Axis.[11] The contrast between word and deed demonstrated that Britain's policy makers were of two minds about what to do with the liberated Italian colonies. One side, composed principally of colonial and military officers, was pessimistic about Ethiopian conditions and political capacities and believed that something approaching a temporary protectorate or at least a period of tutelage was required. The Foreign Office, on the other hand, was far less interested in reform of Ethiopia than in keeping Great Britain's reputation free from suspicion of imperialism. Eden and others in the Foreign Office had faith that Ethiopia could put its own house in order without any form of tutelege.[12]

The British used wartime exigencies to justify their control of "liberated" Ethiopia. The virtual total curtailment of national sovereignty by the British military administration was accepted by the Ethiopian government because it had effectively no way to object. The country was placed unilaterally under an Occupied Enemy Territory Administration (OETA) run from Nairobi, a center of colonial and white-settler rule. The name, OETA, was offensive to Ethiopians who never conceded that their country was lawfully occupied by the Italians.[13] OETA was headed by Sir Philip Mitchell, a South-African-born colonial official, formerly British governor of Uganda, and no friend of African independence. The British occupation under Mitchell's direction was later described by an American observer as being tantamount to a protectorate over Ethiopia.[14]

In British colonial and military circles it was moreover widely assumed, and hoped, that this situation could be rendered permanent. Gordon Waterfield, who was in charge of propaganda in Addis Ababa at that time, recalled:

> British officers in charge of the political administration, a rapidly growing organization, were talking openly of establishing control over Ethiopia on the Sudan model with political officers throughout the country . . . All the old arguments were brought up about the benefits of British control. They did not like to see the Italian improvements, which had cost millions of pounds, go down the drain under an Ethiopian administration; besides that, Ethiopia was regarded as a rich pendant to the Sudan, including as it did Lake Tsana and the source of the Blue Nile.[15]

Such machinations were no doubt bruited about in some quarters in the early years of World War II. But already the "Official Mind of Imperialism" was in decline. Although some officers may have dreamed of expanding the British Empire as well as defeating the Axis powers, countervailing factors antithetical to imperialism were developing during the war.

## THE ANGLO-ETHIOPIAN AGREEMENTS

The Anglo-Ethiopian Agreement of 1942 evidenced the ambivalence of British attitudes toward Ethiopia. This two-year agreement recognized Ethiopian independence but obliged the emperor to make concessions that preserved and legitimized a very substantial degree of British control. The Preamble stated that "the Government of UK recognize that Ethiopia is now a free and independent State and His Majesty the Emperor, Haile Selassie I, is its lawful Ruler." The remaining articles drastically curtailed the practical application of this statement.

The agreement provided for the exchange of ambassadors, with the British minister receiving precedence over any other foreign representative. Various articles formalized firm British controls over the war-time administration of Ethiopia. The Ogaden was to remain under British administration of Somalia, and the British had the right to keep such military forces in Ethiopia as they thought necessary.[16] Under the agreement, units of the British Military Mission to Ethiopia (BMME) and advisors operated throughout the country. Despite infringements of Ethiopian sovereignty, the 1942 agreement marked an important stage in the country's decolonization in that it embodied the first diplomatic recognition of the restoration of Ethiopian independence.

## THE WOYANE REVOLT

The emperor sought to consolidate his reign, often frustrated by the short lead allowed him by the British, who were still fighting a war in Africa. In 1943, the two empires cooperated in a meaningful and far-reaching way, however, when the British helped put down a most serious revolt against Haile Selassie. The "Woyane" revolt arose essentially out of dissatisfaction with the imposition of imperial rule over Tigre province after the war.[17] Supporters of the Woyane faulted the emperor's regime for maladministration, excessive taxation, official corruption, and consequent brigandage.[18] Tigreans were traditional and historic rivals of the more numerous Amharas, the ethnic group of Emperor Haile Selassie. Tigrean nobility, who perceived their position to be endangered by the central government's growth, were joined in armed insurrection by the peasantry, who felt victimized by government officials and their militias. The leaders aspired to separate from Ethiopia and unite with Eritrea, then under British military administration (an arrangement actually recommended by a British Committee on Ethiopia in May 1943 that was rejected by Eden).[19]

For almost five months, the Woyane movement blocked roads and controlled most of Tigre. Units of the new regular Ethiopian army with British advisors were sent to reinforce territorial troops in the area. In the ensuing Battle at Amba Alagi, government forces were attacked by rebel forces of up to 5,000 men. The situation was serious enough for the British advisors to ask for bomber support for the 8,000 government troops and 6,000 territorials. Ammunition was in such short supply that government forces nearly had to retreat. The British Foreign Office believed that this would probably cause the fall of the emperor and judged it necessary to agree to the request for bombers. In addition the British military argued that the north road passing through Amba Alagi was vital to their communications in the continuing war against the Axis.[20]

Three Blenheim bombers from Aden flew a number of missions. On the first runs, only pamphlets containing threats from the emperor and the ichege, the head of the Ethiopian Church, were dropped as the British originally refused to allow bombs to be used. Under pressure to relieve the British advisors and their troops, the RAF eventually carried out bombing raids, culminating in a raid on Makelle where 70 were killed and 200 wounded. Most casualties were noncombatants. The air raids had the desired effect. Government troops were able to advance on Amba Alagi, and the opposition "melted away."

Mopping-up operations were carried out on a broad scale by the Ethiopian military, and their harsh methods created further resentment of imperial rule.[21] The government exiled or imprisoned the leaders of the revolt, and the emperor took reprisals against peasants suspected of supporting the Woyane. The emperor had taken the Woyane movement seriously, since an uprising of this type probably would have received British support had it succeeded.

The Woyane of Tigre have never forgotten the ruthless, indiscriminant punishment inflicted upon their people by the Amhara rulers. When the Woyane came to power in Ethiopia as the TPLF in 1991, their resentment was manifested in official and unofficial discrimination and harassment of the Amhara. Indeed, one aspect of the ethnic federalism of the FDRE is but a thinly disguised license to encourage hatred of the Amharas. The British role in crushing the Woyane revolt and in bombing civilians remains in the collective memory too.

## UNITED STATES INVOLVEMENT

In late 1942, the United States opened a lend-lease center in Eritrea. Commencement of relations with the United States enabled the Ethiopian Government to begin freeing itself from dependence on Great Britain. The emperor received moral support from the United States, a limited amount of technical assistance, and promises of more substantial aid. This ultimately led to the signing of a "Mutual Aid Agreement" between the United States and Ethiopia on 9 August 1943. The Agreement, "planned in Washington, agreed to by Washington, and condoned by London," was a watershed in Ethiopian diplomatic, social, and economic history.[22] The friction with Great Britain generated by the United States becoming the paramount economic power in the Horn and the Middle East underscores the thesis of W. Roger Louis "that the sense of historic antagonism between Britain and the United States continued to exist along with the spirit of cooperation engendered by the war."[23] Emboldened by the American presence, the Ethiopian government demanded termination of its

1942 agreement with Britain. The Allies' concern with defeating the Axis powers loomed more important, however, than American rhetorical anticolonialism or British imperial ambitions. Concord between London and Washington set the stage for a new agreement in Ethiopia and deprived the emperor of diplomatic leverage to play the two powers off against each other.

The ensuing Anglo-Ethiopian Agreement of 1944, signed on 19 December, was generally considered a triumph for Ethiopia.[24] The agreement provided for no special relationship between British advisors and the Ethiopian government and placed the head of the BMME under the authority of the Ethiopian minister of war. Article VII, however, provided for continued British occupation of the Ogaden and Reserved Area in order to contribute to effective prosecution of the war. But World War II soon ended and a Labour government with different ideas about empire came to power in Britain.

At war's end, Ethiopia was surrounded by territories ruled by Britain—except for the small enclave of French Somaliland, her only outlet to the sea. Only seven years later, in 1952, Britain ceased to rule any part of the Horn.

## GREATER SOMALIA

In 1946, while the British were still in military control of the former *Africa Orientale Italiana*, they considered the possibility of "Greater Somalia" as a nation based on ethnic and linguistic frontiers and the principle of self-determination. Clement Attlee, the new Labour prime minister, strongly believed that Britain could not afford further territorial responsibilities, especially in areas such as Somaliland which from the beginning had been "a dead loss."[25] The Colonial Office hoped to alleviate the problems of that deficit area, and at the same time, felt a sense of responsibility for Somalia. The Colonial Office envisioned the creation of a viable territory, a Greater Somalia, composed of British and Italian Somaliland and the Ogaden area of Ethiopia inhabited by Somali people—under a British trusteeship (the Somali areas of Northern Kenya were seldom included in such British plans).[26] Acquisition of the Ogaden had long preoccupied the East African Department because without it the Somalis in British territory were cut off from grazing lands thought vital to their existence.[27]

To the Americans and Soviets, the idea of a Greater Somalia appeared to be military expansion of the British Empire. There was no way that the British could convince the world at large, especially the

Russians, of the purity of British motives in Somalia.[28] The possibility of oil in Italian Somaliland kept alive British interest in gaining a trusteeship over Greater Somalia,[29] but international circumstances would not permit the establishment of a British regime. Failing their own trusteeship of Italian Somaliland, the Colonial Office considered administration by the United Nations, a plan quickly rejected given the danger of Soviet participation. Ultimately the scheme became embroiled in Great Britain's broader foreign policy objectives and specifically British efforts to secure strategic rights in Cyrenaica (in present-day Libya). Reluctantly, the Colonial Office supported Italian trusteeship of the former colony—to solidify United States, French, and Italian backing of British ambitions in Cyrenaica (a ploy muted by Libyan independence in 1948).

The Italian trusteeship was a relatively peaceful ten-year period leading to independence for Italian Somaliland in 1960, when it was united with British Somaliland to form the new nation of Somalia. In 1948, Prime Minister Attlee had announced evacuation of British military administration from Ethiopian territories in the Ogaden. The BMME, with little finance to continue operations, while fearing communist infiltration, nonetheless closed down its office in early 1951. The formal return of the Ogaden to Ethiopia was confirmed by the Anglo-Ethiopian Agreement of 1954. The process of decolonizing Ethiopia, which was considered complete only with the restoration of her internationally recognized pre-1935 frontiers, had taken one and a half decades.

The British legacy, a vision of a Greater Somalia, had inspired young Somali nationalists to bring into being a fatherland of Somali people throughout the Horn. This aspiration in turn led to wars between Somalia and Ethiopia over the disputed Ogaden and to unrest in Kenya. The matter is still far from settled, and the ghost of Greater Somalia, temporarily stilled by the clan-inspired chaos in the remains of Somalia, may well return to haunt Ethiopia and the world in the future.

## THE ERITREAN PROBLEM

In 1943, British officials continued to view the empire as vital and capable of future growth. One strategy was to divide Eritrea, giving the southern part of the former Italian colony to Ethiopia and creating a new Christian Tigre nation on either side of the Eritrean frontier under British protection.[30] This scheme came to nought in the austere realities of the postwar world. The financially strapped British were unwilling to subsidize the territory, but under their tutelage, Eritreans became more politically aware and active. A legislature with elected members chosen from competing political parties was established, a local newspaper began publishing, and there was a modest increase in educational opportunity.[31]

The problem of what to do with the former Italian colony was complicated by, among other things, British designs on Cyrenaica, the muddled situation in Somalia, fears of communist victory in the Italian elections of 1948, and international relations that were evolving along Cold War parameters. The British would have preferred to give the southern part of Eritrea to Ethiopia, and the Moslem north, to the Sudan; but Khartoum declined the offer. The British then considered creating a trusteeship in the territory. Officials of the Foreign Office and Colonial Office were divided on whether to place Eritrea under Italian trusteeship or to give over the area to Ethiopia.[32] Meanwhile, the principal actors were staking their claims.

Ethiopian foreign policy in the late 1940s was mainly concerned with the future of Eritrea, whose integration was considered a matter of major economic and strategic importance. Eritrea's Red Sea ports of Massawa and Asseb would be attractive links to the commerce of landlocked Ethiopia. Above all, to Ethiopia, Eritrea represented the historic route of Italian invasions.[33]

Among Eritreans the Christians of the highlands wanted unity with Ethiopia; the Muslims of the northwest wanted independence. The Unionist Party wanted all of the former colony to be united with Ethiopia. The political opposition wanted an independent Eritrea.[34]

For its part, the Italian government sought restitution of Eritrea, the oldest Italian colony and home of 37,000 Italians (in contrast to Somalia where there were only 5,000 Italians). The Italian position was countered by fear of putting Ethiopia between two Italian pincers in both Somaliland and Eritrea. Labour Foreign Secretary Ernest Bevin did not want to reestablish "Italian rule with British bayonets," and finally, responsibility for the future of Eritrea was passed on to the United Nations.[35]

Britain wanted to keep "anticolonial" Ethiopia out of the U.N. Trusteeship Council and thus did not opt for Ethiopian trusteeship of Eritrea. Ethiopian participation in the Korean War, in which 1,000 Ethiopian troops served with the United Nations, however, convinced American officials that all Eritrea should be federated with Ethiopia.[36] Such a federation would expedite American plans to develop a strategic listening station and other military installations in an Eritrea united with a war-tested, anticommunist ally.

Disposition of the territory was finally decided by the United Nations, and in September 1952, Eritrea officially became "an autonomous state federated with Ethiopia" under the Ethiopian crown. A short time later, Eritrea was absorbed into Ethiopia as just another province. Many Eritreans who had learned respect for parliamentary democracy, pluralist elections, the rule of law, and the protection of human rights under British administration were outraged at their fate of being forced into an authoritarian monarchy.

By 1960, Eritrean liberation movements had developed that were to engulf Ethiopia in a thirty-year civil war. One victor of the war, the Eritrean People's Liberation Front (EPLF), successfully negotiated for a referendum among Eritreans about the future of their state. In April 1993, Eritrean voters overwhelmingly declared for independence. A large number of Ethiopians, however, thought the unilateral separation from Ethiopia, though sanctioned by the Transitional Government of Ethiopia, was illegal. Rancor over an independent Eritrea is one of the most divisive issues in contemporary Ethiopia. Ultimately, the problem will have to be resolved to the satisfaction of the Ethiopian as well as the Eritrean people.

## THE LEGACY OF THE BRITISH EMPIRE IN ETHIOPIA

The British military occupation of Ethiopia and neighboring territories during and immediately after World War II left its mark on the Horn of Africa. Far from being in decline, imperialism and empire were revitalized during the war and in the period of reconstruction which followed.[37] Despite soothing words from Churchill and Eden, Emperor Haile Selassie remained distrustful of British designs on his empire, and indeed, some official minds would have liked a protectorate over Abyssinia.

A presence in the Horn would have been in keeping with strategic postwar plans of Great Britain in the late 1940s when Africa gradually superseded India as one of the ultimate justifications for the existence of the British Empire.[38] In tandem with a Mediterranean base to protect British access to Middle East oil, Bevin envisioned a "belt stretching from West Africa to East Africa" which might offset the cost of retaining a Levantine defense commitment.[39] Bureaucratic inertia also encouraged holding on to the remnants of empire since the chiefs of staff always objected "to evacuating anything where they have been for some time."[40] Die-hard colonialists, heartened by such prospects, championed the idea that Africa in the twentieth century would be as important to the empire as India had been in the nineteenth.

British designs on Ethiopia and the Horn, however, were part of a wider debate within the Labour government from 1945 through 1951. One side, led by Foreign Secretary Bevin, sought to strengthen a British Empire seen as a beneficent force in world affairs. The ideas of these "Imperialists" clashed with those of "Little Englanders," who were more skeptical about Britain's economic and military capacity to remain a "great power."[41] Prime Minister Attlee, more willing than Bevin to acknowledge the diminution of British power, was the leading spokesman for "Little England" sentiments. Attlee urged his colleagues not to make costly military and administrative commitments "for sentimental reasons based on the past."[42]

While Labour leaders wrangled about the future of empire, two developments in the wartime experience of Great Britain were working against any aspirations of the British staying on in the Horn—or almost anywhere else. First, British economic resources were depleted. By the end of the war, Britain had accumulated an overseas debt of £3,355 million and huge deficits in its balance of payments. Subsidization of "deficit areas" was out of the question. Second, British power had experienced relative decline in relation to that of the United States and the Soviet Union.[43]

In Great Britain itself, under the impact of the war, the British people had "ceased to believe in empire."[44] Furthermore, the Atlantic Charter with its associated war to liberate conquered lands from nazism and fascism was not propitious for territorial expansion of the British Empire. With all these factors stacked against further imperial ambitions and with the required levers of power no longer available, the British abandoned the Horn and eventually all of their colonies in Africa.

Instead of settlers and district officers, the British left behind seeds of discord in the rocky passes of Tigre, in Mediterranean-like Asmara, and in the deserts of Somalia. The British military probably kept the "Little Emperor" on his throne in 1943, but the Tigrean Woyane, already contemptuous of Amhara rule, were filled with a new sense of hatred when British officers and air strikes paved the way for draconian punishment of peasants and nobles by Haile Selassie's forces. The emperor did not ask about the justice of the Tigreans' case; it was enough that the rebels had challenged his administration.[45] Today, despite rhetoric to the contrary, ethnic hatred, especially against the Amhara, is one of the driving forces of the government of the Woyane-dominated FDRE.

Other legacies of the British administration were left in Somalia and the Ogaden—and these were to cause problems at a later time. The thwarted ambitions of Greater Somalia have spawned fear, loathing, and war over lands of little worth except for limited grazing. But on the positive side, former British Somaliland constitutes the one extant polity in a country that exists only on maps. In contrast to others, the British apparently taught the inhabitants of their Somali colony how to make government work.

The same can be said of Eritrea. Although the British were there for a relatively short time (from 1941–1952), they instilled in Eritreans an appreciation for, among other things, democratic processes, political parties, a free press, and education. This gave Eritreans a certain panache that developed into arrogance when they were involuntarily joined to the less Anglicized Ethiopians. Resentment against their forced unity with more populous Ethiopia runs deep in the Eritrean inheritors of the benefits of both British occupation and Italian colonialism. Now we await the outcome of an avowedly dictatorial transition to see if Eritreans really remember the lessons inculcated in them by the British fifty years ago.

For most of the Ethiopians, Eritreans, and Somalis who were yet unborn when the British left their lands, the hatreds and distrusts of their neighbors in the Horn have existed so long as to seem generic. What many of them have forgotten is the catalytic impact of British rule and administration on their present-day quandaries. The brief British occupation of Ethiopia and neighboring areas from 1941–1952 left its indelible marks on the Horn of Africa.

## REFERENCES


1. See, e.g., Theodore M. Vestal, "Democratic Deficits in the Transitional Government," *Ethiopian Review*, July 1994; "Deficits of Democracy in the Transitional Government of Ethiopia Since 1991," in Harold G. Marcus, ed., *New Trends in Ethiopian Studies*, vol. 2 (Lawrenceville, NJ: Red Sea Press, 1994), 188–204; "An Analysis of the New Constitution of Ethiopia and the Process of Its Adoption," *Ethiopian Register*, December 1994; January, February 1995); "The Precious Comb-Box (*Yemabetteria Muday*) of Ethiopia: An Analysis of the Rule of the Transitional Government of Ethiopia and Its Legacy for the Future," *Ethiopian Register*, August, September 1995).
2. Ronald Robinson and John Gallagher, *Africa and the Victorians* (New York: St. Martin's, 1961), 289.
3. Elizabeth Monroe, *Britain's Moment in the Middle East 1914–1956* (Baltimore: Johns Hopkins Press, 1963), 11.
4. Peter J. Yeargood, "Great Britain and the Repartition of Africa, 1914–19," *Journal of Imperial and Commonwealth History*, 18 (1990): 316–341.

5. Alan Moorehead, *Mediteranean Front* (London: Hamish Hamilton, 1941), 37.

6. Public Record Office, Foreign Office, 371/24645/306.

7. Leonard Mosley, *Haile Selassie The Conquering Lion* (London: Weidenfeld and Nicolson, 1964), 260. Margaret Perham criticizes Mosley's depiction of British colonial ambitions in Ethiopia as "somewhat sinister" and "somewhat inadequately documented." She infers that such intrigue could not be taken as a common British practice of the era. Margaret Perham, *The Government of Ethiopia* (Evanston, IL: Northwestern Univ. Press, 1969), xxix.

8. Richard Pankhurst, "Decolonization of Ethiopia, 1940–55," *Decolonization of Africa: Southern Africa and the Horn of Africa* (Paris: UNESCO, 1981), 119–132.

9. Mosley, 273.

10. Michael Crowder, "The Course of the War on African Soil," *The Cambridge History of Africa*, Michael Crowder (ed.), Vol. 8 (Cambridge: Cambridge Univ. Press, 1984), 16.

11. Pankhurst, 123.

12. Margaret Perham, *The Government of Ethiopia* (Evanston, IL: Northwestern Univ. Press, 1969), 392.

13. David Shirreff, *Bare Feet and Bandoliers: Wingate, Sanford, the Patriots and the Part They Played in the Liberation of Ethiopia* (London: Radcliffe Press, 1995), 275.

14. John H. Spencer, *Ethiopia, the Horn of Africa and U.S. Policy* (Cambridge, MA: Institute for Foreign Policy Analysis, 1977), 9. Mitchell was recalled in June 1942 to the Colonial Service as Governor of Fiji and High Commissioner for the Western Pacific. One wonders if he was promoted to get him away from Ethiopia and conflicts with the emperor. After the war, Mitchell described Ethiopia as a "glaring example of what premature political independence means in suffering, misery and degradation for the mass of the people when it is no more than the independence of a small group of competing political factions at the centre to do what they like to the mass of the people, who have neither the understanding nor the local institutions within their control to enable them to protect themselves . . . " "Local Governments: despatch from Sir P. Mitchell (Kenya) to Mr. Creech Jones (secretary of state), commenting on the circular despatch," CO 847/3516, no. 88 (30 May 1947).

15. Mosley, 275.

16. Rennell of Rodd, *British Military Administration of Occupied Territories* (London: HMSO, 1948), 539–43.

17. John W. Turner, "Historical Setting," in Thomas P. Ofcansky and LaVerle Berry (eds.), *Ethiopia: A Country Study*, (Washington, DC: Library of Congress, 1993), 48.

18. Harold Marcus, *A History of Ethiopia* (Berkeley: Univ. of California Press, 1994), 154.

19. Harold Marcus, *The Politics of Empire: Ethiopia, Great Britain and the United States* (Lawrenceville, NJ: Red Sea Press, 1995), 22.

20. Patrick Gilkes, *The Dying Lion* (London: Julian Friedmann, 1975), 189.

21. Christopher Clapham, "The Horn of Africa," in Michael Crowder (ed.),

*The Cambridge History of Africa*, Vol. 8 (Cambridge: Cambridge Univ. Press, 1984), 48.

22. Harold Marcus, *The Politics of Empire: Ethiopia, Great Britain and the United States* (Lawrenceville, NJ: Red Sea Press, 1995), 21.

23. Wm. Roger Louis, *Imperialism at Bay* (Oxford: Oxford Univ. Press, 1977), 7.

24. Marcus, *The Politics of Empire*, 39.

25. Memorandum by Attlee, 1 Sep 1945, C.P. (45) 144, CAB 129/1. In Mussolini's *Africa Orientale Italiana*, for the first time the great majority of Somalis were brought under common rule.

26. Wm. Roger Louis, *The British Empire in the Middle East 1945–1951* (Oxford: Clarendon Press, 1984), 274–75.

27. Louis, 282.

28. Louis, 281.

29. "Somaliland Protectorate and the Horn of Africa," Cabinet memo by Lennox-Boyd advocating the creation of a Greater Somalia, CP (56) 180, 25 July 1956, CAB 129/82.

30. Committee on Ethiopia, "Report on Future Policy Towards Ethiopia," Cairo, 18 May 1943, cited in Marcus, *Politics*, 22.

31. Margaret Perham, *The Government of Ethiopia* (Evanston, IL: Northwestern Univ. Press, 1969), xxxi.

32. Wm. Roger Louis, *The British Empire in the Middle East 1945–1951* (Oxford: Clarendon Press, 1984), 290.

33. Louis, 289.

34. Louis, 290.

35. Defence Committee DO (48), 14th Meeting, Top Secret, 30 July 1948, CAB 131/5. Quoted in Louis, *The British Empire in the Middle East 1945–1951*, 294.

36. Marcus, *The Politics of Empire*, 77.

37. P. J. Cain and A. G. Hopkins, *British Imperialism: Crisis and Deconstruction 1914–1990* (London: Longman, 1993), 290.

38. Wm. Roger Louis, *The British Empire in the Middle East 1945–1951* (Oxford: Clarendon Press, 1984), 16.

39. Defence Committee DO (46) 10, 5 April 1946, CAB 131/1.

40. Minute by Oliver Harvey, 3 Nov 1947, FO 371/67084.

41. Wm. Roger Louis, *The British Empire in the Middle East 1945–1951* (Oxford: Clarendon Press, 1984), 4–6.

42. Louis, 275.

43. Wm. Roger Louis, *Imperialism at Bay* (Oxford: Oxford Univ. Press, 1977), 25.

44. A. N. Porter and A. J. Stockwell, *British Imperial Policy and Decolonization, 1938–64* (New York: St. Martin's, 1987), 25.

45. Marcus, *A History of Ethiopia*, 154.

# 4
# THE ADEN FEDERATION
## John Allgood

During the decade of the 1950s, Britain faced a dilemma in the Middle East. Maintaining Britain's primary base at Suez grew increasingly untenable against the rising tide of Egyptian nationalism. To counter this situation, Britain looked to the small Crown Colony of Aden and the hodgepodge of tribal states in the hinterland known as the Aden Protectorates located on the southern tip of the Arabian Peninsula and now part of Yemen. In an effort to strengthen this loose entity British colonial officials initiated a policy in 1952 aimed toward a federation of the Aden Protectorates.[1] The British Empire had achieved mixed success with federation building. Canada, Australia, and South Africa were examples of successful federations, while the proposed Central African Federation of North and South Rhodesia and Nyasaland were failures. Aden lies somewhere in between, never having achieved its intended purpose of securing continued British presence in the region. The creation of the federation in 1959 marks a turning point for the British presence in South Arabia. Even though it did succeed in unifying the region, the federation ultimately failed when, by 1967, Britain was pushed out of South Arabia and later in 1971 announced her withdrawal from the Persian Gulf.

In early 1952, the British hoped federation would achieve two main goals. Theoretically, it would lead toward eventual self-rule. Pragmatically, it would help to maintain British preeminence in South Arabia by deflecting the growth of Arab nationalism. Like most federal schemes in the British Empire, the protectorate federation's main purpose was to create a viable state that would maintain British military and economic influence. With the impending withdrawal from Suez, Aden became increasingly important as a base to protect Britain's commitments to the oil-rich states of the Persian Gulf. Economically, Aden also became more important due to the oil refinery built there by British Petroleum to replace the refineries nationalized by Iran in 1951. A continuous supply of petroleum, either in the form of crude oil from the Persian Gulf or refined gasoline from the British Petroleum refinery, was vital to a Britain facing financial crises following the Second World War.[2] Given such financial and geopolitical considerations Aden now became an essential part of the empire.

A major force behind the federal plan was Kennedy Trevaskis, a junior political officer in the Western Aden Protectorate. Trevaskis had joined the Colonial Service in 1950 and spent his first years as a district officer in Northern Rhodesia. He viewed postwar colonial policy in Africa as blindly implementing "the cliché that self-government was better than good government." Trevaskis saw this view as undermining "our mission" to equip the colonies for independence by establishing "British standards of government."[3] Out of disgust with the course of direct colonial administration, he transferred to the Western Aden Protectorate in 1951 where he was appointed a political officer. His move stemmed from discussion with another colonial officer stationed in the Aden Protectorate who described his duties thusly: "We only advise. We have never governed the Arabs and I doubt whether we ever could."[4] Trevaskis felt that attempts at direct British rule would inevitably lead to a complete loss of British influence and, more important, British prestige in the Middle East. Trevaskis believed that promoting federation would ease the eventual transfer of power in Aden and that "ruling" the territory would only further Arab resentment of British control and condescension, resulting in a speedy British withdrawal and lingering bitterness.

Aden's governor, Sir Tom Hickinbotham, approved Trevaskis's idea for federation in 1952 and set the proposal in motion.[5] Although supported by Hickinbotham, the plan for federation was primarily the creation of Trevaskis. He completed a preliminary constitution by late 1952. This constitution proposed two federations, one in the Eastern and the other in the Western Protectorate with each federation containing an executive and a legislative council and a single high commissioner performing the duties presently undertaken by the governor. Hickinbotham sent the completed document to the Colonial Office, noting that federation would serve three aims. First, it would increase political solidarity in the protectorate and help bind the region to Aden Colony. Second, it would train the population for self-government. Last, and probably the most important to Whitehall, a federation would eventually reduce British costs in Aden by creating an economically independent state. Hickinbotham emphasized the argument for federation by stating: "It is our avowed policy to train the local people in this Colony and Protectorate to be able to manage their own affairs . . . but we are not doing so quickly enough nor as wholeheartedly as I could wish." Apparently this statement made the crucial difference since the Secretary of State for Colonies, Oliver Lyttleton, commented in the margin, "This from Hick!"[6]

Colonial Office officials in London were both impressed and amazed. Minutes circulated within the Central Africa and Aden Departments demanding reactions and criticism. The proposal met with complete agreement and support.[7] Trevaskis's proposals were favored in the Colonial Office for reasons similar to Hickinbotham's conclusions; however, the Colonial Office primarily felt that federation would enable the British to further their control of the region while placating the nationalist fervor that seemed to run rampant across the Middle East. These reactions directly contrast with Trevaskis's intended goals. Trevaskis intended to advise, and he viewed the move to federation as the fulfillment of self-government. In contrast, the Colonial Office understood the plan to be an affirmation of Britain's ultimate authority.

Although supported by the Colonial Office, Whitehall realized the problems with the scheme. One of these was to convince the other governmental offices, primarily the Foreign Office, of the plan's suitability. Not that Foreign Office protests could kill the federation, but the Colonial Office should "find out what the Foreign Office objections are and satisfy ourselves that they are not valid."[8] The main comment of the Foreign Office about the federation emphasized that the Imam of Yemen would respond negatively to the proposal.[9] The Imam still considered the Aden Protectorates to be part of his historic territory and was unmoved by the fact that the region had not actually been under the control of the Zaidi Imamate for over two hundred years. Despite concerns about Yemen, the Foreign Office approved the scheme. Although the Colonial Office readily approved the proposals for federation, the department heads of the Colonial Office concerned themselves with the local reaction to the plan's announcement. One Colonial Office administrator thought the plan should be implemented as quickly as possible since "the Protectorate Rulers are fickle and inclined to be suspicious of Her Majesty's Government and of each other."[10]

By early January 1954 the plan became public knowledge. Until that point, Trevaskis had systematically promoted his scheme behind the scenes until he was confident of its public support. Governor Hickinbotham called the rulers of the protectorate to a meeting to unveil the proposal. The response from the protectorate rulers seemed favorable to the colonial officials and the governor requested further consultation with the rulers.[11] As expected, the Imam of Yemen opposed the plan. In February 1954, a delegation from the Arab League, led by the Secretary-General, Abdul Khaliq Hassuna, met with Hickinbotham to protest the proposed federation. The delegation favored the Yemeni position that the federal plan violated the 1934 Treaty of Sana by attempting to change the existing situation in the protectorate. In response, Hickinbotham, following Colonial Office directions, stood firm on the issue and emphasized that the success or failure for federation lay solely in the hands of the protectorate rulers.[12] Rebuffed by Hickinbotham, the Arab League passed a resolution requesting the protectorate rulers to reject the federation because it conflicted with the spirit of Arab, and more specifically Yemeni, nationalism.[13] The most influential ruler of the protectorates, Sultan Ali of Lahej, when asked by Trevaskis for his feelings, responded that "[the proposals] were like surrender terms dictated to a defeated enemy! Do you think we want to become a colony of yours?"[14] After this bitter denunciation, the British quickly adopted a less aggressive stance toward the project, obliging Hickinbotham to "soft pedal" the idea and not press on at full steam.

With little support for federation the Colonial Office found it necessary to revaluate the situation for Anthony Eden, who had recently succeeded Winston Churchill as the prime minister. Until this point, no other far-reaching proposals had been available concerning the federation. The study, "Long Range Policy on Aden and the Protectorates," completed in September 1955 marked the result of Colonial Office thinking on Aden. Briefly, the document emphasized Aden's strategic importance to Britain's position east of Suez, especially in the Persian Gulf.[15] To Whitehall, the strategic, economic, and diplomatic reasons for staying far outweighed the setbacks of losing the colony to self-rule. Of the three factors, the strategic was of dubious value to the Colonial Office, the economic was more important, and the diplomatic was most important. The diplomatic importance of Aden could be distilled into one word: prestige. Britain's influence in the area amounted to a guarantee of previous promises to the leaders in the protectorate as well as promises to the far more essential states in the Persian Gulf. To London, Aden's permanent position in the empire must be emphasized to the colony and protectorate; any other alternative would give false hopes to the inhabitants of the region.

While officials in London examined policy for colony and protectorate, the governor continued to support federation. In April 1956,

Hickinbotham officially repeated the British desire for federation during a conference with the protectorate rulers. Because of his instruction to slow the process of federation, Hickinbotham's proposal featured lukewarm, bureaucratic reassurances that stressed the need in the protectorate for "close association." Hickinbotham distanced the British from initiating the process while giving the rulers "complete freedom among themselves to choose or reject any proposals" leading to such a federation. The governor wanted federation, but Whitehall, fearful of alienating the rulers, discouraged any direct British manipulations.[16] As before, the rulers' responses were vaguely optimistic, but they still did not completely accept the plan.

A trip by Undersecretary of State for the Colonies, Lord Lloyd, to Aden in 1956 resulted from the long-range policy on Aden. Lloyd intended to clearly enunciate the goals of the policy both to the governor and the leaders in the colony and protectorate. In a speech in June 1956 he stated:

> [I]t would not be reasonable or sensible, or indeed in the interests of the Colony's inhabitants, for them to aspire to any aim beyond that of a considerable degree of internal self-government. . . . [Britain] cannot foresee the possibility of any fundamental relaxation of their responsibilities for the Colony.[17]

Whitehall hoped that this statement would confirm the continuing position of Britain in the region. The Colonial Office believed that "this step [federation], far from increasing the risk of trouble, might have the effect of reducing it."[18] None of the leading British officials, above all Hickinbotham, intended for the federation to lead to independence. To reassure the Secretary of State for Colonies, Lennox-Boyd, Hickinbotham emphasized,

> *As regards independence, that was an absurd idea and should be put out of mind forthwith* for the only reasonable goal to aim for was some degree of internal self-government and the speed of realization of that goal and the actual degree of internal self-government must depend on the political responsibility displayed by the people and their leaders, which is sadly lacking in both at the present.[19]

This statement summed up British goals for the federation and was praised by Lennox-Boyd as "robust words . . . [that] are entirely to my liking and certainly need saying."[20] The federation gave the Colonial Office a means to maintain British preeminence. British determination only increased after the Suez disaster.

Lord Lloyd's statement to the colony leaders, intended to reduce any feeling of nationalism in the region, actually caused resentments and animosity in the colony and protectorate. His uncompromising declaration of British resolve had the opposite of its intended effect; protectorate rulers became convinced that Britain's power in the region was declining. This perception is evident in one protectorate ruler's conversation with Lord Lloyd in which he labeled Britain the "Sick Old Woman of the Middle East."[21] Progress on federation also stalled in August 1956 when Hickinbotham was replaced by Sir William Luce.[22] Understandably, Luce held his own ideas about what best suited the region, and British policy toward Aden soon took another direction.

The Suez crisis in late 1956 removed the initiative from British policy makers and helped create a new position for Aden. Previously, the Colonial Office tried to limit, as much as possible, Aden's use as a military base.[23] Now the failed Anglo-French invasion of Egypt in late 1956 caused Aden to become the center of British commitments in the Middle East.[24]

The Suez crisis also led to the formation of a new Conservative government in London under Harold Macmillan in early 1957. Duncan Sandys, minister of defence, immediately went to work to try to rearrange Britain's defense policies after the loss of Suez while maintaining Britain's position overseas. The White Paper of 1957 was the initial outcome of Sandys's labors and made specific reference to the continued role of Aden in the empire stating, "Britain must at all times be ready to defend Aden Colony and Protectorates and the territories on the Persian Gulf for whose defence she is responsible."[25] This defense guarantee forced Britain to expand her role in Aden and helped drastically change the political climate there.

Although the replacement of Sir Tom Hickinbotham by Sir William Luce in August 1956 occurred before the fiasco in Suez, the transition from Hickinbotham to Luce in terms of policy did not occur until 1957. Luce brought a new focus for policy toward Aden and the protectorates. Kennedy Trevaskis thought Luce's method of "looking, listening and taking note" was highly effective and that he "soon knew a great deal more about South Arabia than many of his closest advisors."[26] Through this informal style, Luce quickly came to different conclusions concerning future policy in the area. Luce proposed a new path of increased "Adenisation" of the Civil Service and a more intensive economic development scheme for the protectorate.[27] Although Luce's suggestions implied few concrete goals when initially submitted, they met with some support in the Colonial Office because they allowed Britain to regain the initiative lost after Suez. They also allowed the British to redevelop the systems of internal collaboration in the colony and protectorate without either actively promoting or killing the federation.

As discussions over the developmental proposal progressed, colonial officials began to define more precisely the value of Aden colony and the protectorate within the empire. One Colonial Office official summed up the prevalent view:

> The whole policy basis of these proposals [development] is one of *defence*. For strategic, commercial and diplomatic reasons Great Britain needs to retain the Colony; the retention of the Colony is rendered very much easier (and perhaps even only rendered possible) by retention of control of the Protectorate; various devices for maintaining our control of the Protectorate have been tried, including military measures and the political dodge "Federation"; these steps are in varying degrees unsatisfactory or expensive; the recommended means of retaining control of the Protectorate is to associate the people of the Protectorate with the West by economic and social development; and this has to be paid for.[28]

The port of Aden retained its major economic value, and by the late 1950s it was second only to New York in volume of goods handled, but little else existed economically outside of the port. To Luce, political development depended on economic development in the region, and the protectorate was materially and politically poor in the eyes of the governor as well as everyone else. Luce believed Trevaskis's plan tried to put the cart before the horse and the outcome would be disastrous.[29] In contrast, Luce's plan had certain drawbacks for the rest of Whitehall; it would cost more money and would entail a more concentrated political effort in the region since increased internal development required additional British economic advisors, especially in agriculture.[30]

The Colonial Office reaction focused on two beliefs: first, that the man on the scene was more knowledgeable of the situation in Aden and the protectorate; second and most important, that the end product of British policy in South Arabia rested on the maintenance of British preeminence in the region. The main problem with the development proposals was financial. The Colonial Office viewed the developmental scheme as "the recommended means of retaining control of the Protectorate," but it wondered where the money would come from.[31] To sound out Treasury opinion, Colonial Office officials in London forwarded Luce's vague developmental proposals to them. Although Treasury did not reject the proposals outright, it requested a more detailed explanation. Most important, Treasury sidestepped the financial problem by suggesting that "some of the finance [come] from

C.D. and W. [Commonwealth Development and Welfare] sources."[32] At the same time, Luce felt he had to "insist on being given the opportunity of choosing where the cuts should be made."[33] Treasury would not allow any "excessive" expenditure in the region unless absolutely necessary. To the Treasury Office, Aden remained a minor bastion of the British Empire and resources directed there could easily prove to be wasted investment.

Even with Treasury objections, the development plan had a strong supporter in Harold Macmillan who wholeheartedly agreed to the change in policy toward Aden. When informed of the shift from federation to development, Macmillan emphasized that "I always thought this policy [federation] was wrong."[34] Macmillan gave his support even though the costs for the development plan had increased. The main obstacle remained Treasury, which wanted to know where the funds to pay for development would come from. Aden, and especially the protectorate, remained a very poor region. The only real income for the region rested on the port trade located entirely in Aden. Because the colony and protectorate were officially separate entities and the protectorate desperately needed money to develop, the money had to come from Britain.

As a compromise that would keep alive the development plan in theory, Luce agreed to move the timetable from the 1958–59 fiscal year to the 1959–60 fiscal year. The strong belief by Luce and the Colonial Office in the development plan is best summed up in the following memorandum:

> It is possible that owing to the alleged poverty [of Britain] the answer of the Ministers to the Governor's proposals will have to be No, or at any rate "No for some time". If they so decide, they should realise the dangers inherent in the alternative. The policy of federation . . . is just not working; we are left with the "carry on" policy; there is nothing in this policy to attract the interests of either the Rulers or the people in the Protectorate, nor to rebut the pretensions of the Yemen or Saudi Arabia; therefore the position on the boundaries and in respect of subversion within the Protectorate, is bound to get more and more difficult. . . . At the same time, the means of dealing with those difficulties are likely to become less and less effective, because the Protectorate officers are slowly being worn out by the present policy of essentially military defence . . . [35]

To Luce and other officials directly concerned with Aden and the protectorate, the development plan provided the British government with increased economic control over the region. At the same time, economic development was viewed as a method of heading off future unrest by improving the welfare of South Arabia.

Although British officials viewed development in Aden and the protectorate with favor, the previous policy of federation was not officially abandoned. British colonial administrators supported federation, but only a federation initiated by the rulers of the protectorate themselves. Britain's policy in South Arabia soon returned to federation thanks to the request in February 1958 by three rulers in the Western Protectorate: the Sharif Hussein of Beihan, the Sultan Saleh of Audhali and the Sultan Ahmed of Fadhli. These rulers pressed forward with the project of federation mainly out of fear of an increasingly powerful Yemen.[36] On 17 January 1958, Egypt and Syria had announced the formation of the United Arab Republic, set for 1 February.[37] Soon afterward, the Imam of Yemen loosely associated his country into the new organization as a part of the United Arab States. The sudden apparent increase in Yemeni power, due to its new close ties with the UAR, added to the danger of an already aggressive Yemen in the eyes of many protectorate rulers. Their request surprised the governor and revived the issue of political development.

Although the British had previously pledged in 1954 that federation was the ultimate aim of British policy in the region, until 1958 Luce had downplayed the federation's importance. Now, in the face of the rulers' request, Luce tried to rebuild support for the idea. Luce sent the first in a series of three letters to the Colonial Office covering the "almost bewildering series of changes which have taken place . . . during the last two or three years" and giving his recommendations for future policy.

> Aden is in the grip of four powerful currents in the tide of world affairs. One is the evolution of the Colonial Empire from dependence to independence, either within or outside the Commonwealth, the second is Arab nationalism, the third is the decline of British power and the fourth is Russian expansionism. All these currents flow towards the same point, that is to say, the termination of British control in Aden.[38]

These were bold words harshly evaluating the future of Britain in the region. To Luce, the British position in South Arabia needed serious reconsideration or drastic consequences would result.

With the request for federation by the states of Beihan, Audhali, and Fadhli the prospects looked better for British influence in South Arabia. Even so, the plan needed significant British support. Luce argued that to make the federation work there needed to be a new treaty relationship so that the ensuing entity would "not appear to be perpetuating the present situation under a new guise"; the federation "must be given teeth" with a strong federal army created from the Aden protectorate levies; finally, and in keeping with Luce's own ideas of economic development, the new federation would need "substantial financial assistance" to build up a stable, independent state. Although these three steps would be costly in terms of time, money, and energy, Luce felt "firmly convinced that we must not let this opportunity slip of encouraging our friends in their aspirations."[39]

The rulers' move to federate independently also met with favor among many Colonial advisors in the area, especially Kennedy Trevaskis, by then the British agent in the Western Aden Protectorate. According to Trevaskis, the rulers showed their desire to overcome the "tribalism" of the past and create a modern nation. Trevaskis felt the only alternative to federal unity was the emergence of an authoritarian "Prussian" state; the only candidate for such a state was Lahej, already on shaky ground with Britain.[40] In 1958, the governor ordered the arrest of Mohammed al-Jifri, head of the South Arabian League and friend of the Lahej Sultan Ali. According to the British, al-Jifri and his two brothers were wanted for meeting "with certain foreign Powers, . . . on behalf of whom they were disrupting the good relations of Her Majesty's Government and the rulers and peoples of the Aden protectorates."[41] Although the two brothers were arrested, Mohammed al-Jifri eluded capture and British relations with Lahej deteriorated.

While hostility began to build in Lahej, the Imam of Yemen stepped up pressure in other parts of the protectorate, especially in Beihan. Since the meeting with Sultan Hussein of Beihan and the other protectorate rulers favoring federation with Luce in February, the Imam had encouraged border incidents in Beihan. As security along the Yemen border destabilized, the governor thought it necessary to increase the British military presence in the protectorate. By March the British garrison in Aden was strengthened by the arrival of two armored car squadrons of the Life Guards.[42] Further events in Yemen caused heightened concern about the military problem in the protectorate. Soviet influence in Yemen gained strength. The construction of a Yemeni port at Ras el Khatib by Soviet engineers, ostensibly for commercial purposes but feared as a possible naval base for Soviet submarines,[43] underlined Luce's previous comment to the Colonial Office about "the dangers of Russian Imperialism."[44] In response to these perceived dangers and to aid in the search for Mohammed al-Jifri, the British also sent two infantry companies from Aden into Lahej. Ali protested the uninvited military presence in his state, claiming that the British actions "terrified" his people and expressing shock to the *Times* correspondent over Britain's handling of the matter.[45]

With concerns over the situation in the protectorate, the Colonial Office felt that it was necessary to delay entry of Aden into the proposed federation. This tactic was to allow the federation to gain a more stable government foundation that would be more readily accepted by the Adenis. At the same time, the situation in Aden was not under control. The Aden Trade Unions Congress (ATUC), formed in 1952, grew increasingly radical after learning the power of strikes in 1956.[46] The power of the ATUC grew even more significantly by 1958, with its membership consisting mainly of migrant workers from Yemen. On 23 April 1958, the ATUC called a 24-hour strike. Soon after, a series of bomb attacks struck Aden, which the British felt were directed by elements of the ATUC. These attacks forced Governor Luce to declare a state of emergency in the colony on 2 May 1958. Many, including Trevaskis, saw the bombing as a terrorist protest against the advance toward federation in the protectorate. These terrorist activities were intended to undermine the proposed union because the ATUC opposed the British plan of eventually handing control of Aden to a federation dominated by rulers in the protectorate. With unrest in Aden itself, Colonial Office officials were concerned over the long-term status of the colony vis-a-vis Britain. This was particularly troublesome because Aden was a crown colony; constitutionally this meant it occupied British soil. In addition, the importance of Aden's military potential had grown as Britain's presence in the Middle East declined. Fully aware of the difficulties in Aden, a minister at the time told Trevaskis that "if the states federate, they will immediately want Aden; then, independence; and then where will we be?"[47]

Even with reservations about the future of Aden in the federation, progress continued toward establishment of the federation. By May, supporters of federation grew to include the Amir of Dhala. The British felt the Dathina Council and the Saqladi Sheikh of Shuaib also would join soon thereafter. As talks progressed, the rulers grew concerned over the timing of any proposed federation which they believed might unleash "a torrent of violent abuse from Cairo and Sana'a," the capital of North Yemen. As a result, they argued that establishment of their federation should come as quickly as possible after its announcement.[48] Inevitably, initial talks included lengthy discussions concerning financial support for the new state. The federal plan would entail a dramatically increased British expenditure for the states. Although these figures could and would be easily changed, the one-time British cost for creation of the federation was given as something between £320,000 and £360,000.[49] The recurrent costs for Britain to maintain the new state were even more significant, totaling between £742,000 and £977,000, with most resources going toward support for a National Guard.[50] Although these figures were in their roughest and probably lowest levels during these early talks, they show a dramatic increase in estimates of British expenditure for the burgeoning federation.

Plans went forward in the latter part of 1958 for the establishment of the federation in the protectorates. The three rulers who had requested the federation in January were now joined by the rulers of Dhala and Dathina. One by one, the rulers went to London to hammer out the details and to seek guarantees of military and economic help from Britain for the new scheme.[51] At the same time, the prime minister made expressly clear to British participants that, "we must get rid of this terrible word 'independence.'" From the defense perspective, the ultimate control of Aden by Britain was of paramount interest. In the long term, federation meant "home rule" and little else to the prime minister.[52] To ensure the conference's success, the Colonial Office tried to add as much official ceremony as possible without further alienating the sultan of Lahej, who was also in London at the time but who "could not be trusted" with respect to the federation in its present form.[53]

Initial meetings of the conference focused on the precise amount of money the British government intended to give the federation for start-up costs. The Colonial Office offered the figures previously discussed with Luce in May while the protectorate rulers favored a figure of almost £3 million per annum, nearly double the original offer. Secretary of State for Colonies, Lennox-Boyd, wrote to Heathcoat Amory, Chancellor of the Exchequer, emphasizing that "it is obvious that at the initiation of federal institutions, . . . generosity from Her Majesty's Government . . . is a *sine qua non*."[54] To Heathcoat Amory, the figures meant an additional £1.8 million expenditure from an already tight budget. In addition, it would be "most unwise at this stage to give the Rulers the impression that we will agree to whatever they ask."[55] Although Amory's response was in many respects justified, Lennox-Boyd felt it necessary to immediately reemphasize the importance of a strong financial commitment by Britain. In his own words,

> If we cannot close on these figures, and that [*sic*] quickly, I am terribly afraid that the Federation, if it starts at all, will not start with that feeling of confidence which will be so essential to it in its precarious early days. I beg you to help me over this.[56]

From the perspective of the Colonial Office, the federation thus required near complete financial support in order to maintain British interests in South Arabia. To gain this financial commitment, Lennox-Boyd drafted a note informing the prime minister of the disagreement between the Colonial Office and Treasury. Lennox-Boyd emphasized that by short-changing the federation "we may end by spoiling the launching of the Federation, with all that would mean for our position in Southern Arabia, for a comparatively small sum of money."[57] Eventually, Treasury reluctantly offered an amount that was slightly higher than the previous low figure.

While the rulers negotiated for economic aid and their future position in London, the Iraqi revolution broke out on 14 July 1959. The unstable situation in Iraq and the news of the deaths of the Iraqi royal family caused alarm among the protectorate rulers. In a meeting on 15 July, the colonial secretary emphasized Britain's intent to remain in the region; any intention of withdrawal meant "disaster for all our friends and ruin for ourselves." Assured by his statements, the protectorate rulers accepted the new financial proposals with little discontent. The sharif of Beihan summed up their position on the aid proposals: "if the matters had stood where they were very recently, . . . there would have been strong argument but the events of the last two days had raised difficulties for all." As a result, the rulers judged "it was their duty to say that they were all agreed to the figures of aid offered."[58]

The plan for federation appeared nearly complete, and events in the protectorate removed the most vocal opponent to the plan, the sultan Ali of Lahej. For the past months, Ali had raised objections to the federation on the grounds that it was not wanted by his people and that it was "creating hell" for the region.[59] In protest against the federation, Ali sent the commander of the Lahej armed forces to Yemen to form a liberation army. In response the British called upon the Lahej electoral college to depose and replace Ali on the grounds that this action violated his treaty obligation to abstain from involvement with a foreign power without informing the British.[60] Although this step removed an unsupportive member of the federation from the protectorate, this action, as *The Times* stated, was "apt to have serious consequences" and the explanation for removing the sultan was "rather too thin to stand up to hostile propaganda."[61]

After weeks of negotiating, the plans for federation met with success and the sharif of Beihan, acting as spokesman, expressed his satisfaction to *The Times*.[62] This marked the true beginning of the federation. Overcoming concern over a loss of control in Aden, Whitehall felt that to offer federation at this point would reduce the possibilities of another humiliating colonial failure as experienced in Egypt. But support for the federation was still not universal in Whitehall. One obstacle to the plan remained the military element. The base in Aden was still Britain's most important military position in the region, and the threat posed by Nasser still loomed over the horizon, especially in the wake of the Iraqi coup and the unrest in Jordan. Furthermore, unrest created by the Imam, although subdued since the early part of the year, was still simmering. To the chiefs of staff, federation would result in the loss of British control within two to three years, which meant in turn that Aden could not continue as military base. For the military, the loss of Aden would mean a complete rethinking of the British presence in the Middle East.[63] Yet another base would be abandoned, and the costs for a military presence in the region would continue to rise. Even so, the federation advanced.

On 11 February 1959, the six states formally proclaimed the Federation of the Arab Emirates of the South. In order to show Britain's strong support, a large ceremony was planned. Attending the ceremony were Secretary of State for the Colonies Lennox-Boyd and Governor Luce. Under agreements concluded the previous year, Great Britain agreed to provide military and economic support for the new state. Most of the Colonial Office viewed the new federation as the initial step in completing the political stabilization of the protectorates and Aden Colony. Lennox-Boyd emphasized these hopes in his speech at the ceremony by stating, "It is my earnest hope that while growing in strength the young Federation will also grow in size, and that it will not be long before other States in the Protectorate join it."[64]

Lennox-Boyd's immediate hopes were fulfilled since the federation eventually included all but four states in the protectorate, but nonetheless the federation never really succeeded. Lack of any real financial commitment by Britain remained a liability. The federation never held any strong support inside the protectorate since the ruling council of the federation was led by a different ruler each year. At the same time, the close cooperation of the federation with the British government provided an easy target for nationalist leaders looking for "stooges." In the end, the weakness of the new regime easily outweighed its strengths. The period following the federation's creation is marked by a revolutionary reaction to the federation culminating in British withdrawal in 1967. What was once the federation became the People's Republic of South Yemen, an avowed Marxist state which quickly cut any ties to the old imperial power.[65]

Looking back, Britain's attempt to create a federation in South Arabia may appear to have been fruitless. The British Empire is frequently seen as a repressive and counterproductive force in history;

however, what is often overlooked is the belief, held by many members of the British colonial services, in the beneficial legacy of British rule to the empire. Britain brought order, government, and unity to large regions of the world. How Britain had acquired her empire was largely irrelevant to the Colonial Office. Britain's colonial legacy was important, and the decolonization period is marked by attempts to preserve British institutions and influence. The Aden federation was such an attempt. Although speculative history is a risky and shaky affair, had the federation succeeded and had Britain maintained her dominance in the Persian Gulf, the region might be a different and possibly more stable place today.

## REFERENCES

1. A brief introductory work on the region is Robert Stookey, *South Yemen: A Marxist Republic in Arabia* (Boulder: Westview Press, 1982). More specific on the British presence in Aden is R. J. Gavin, *Aden Under British Rule 1839–1967* (London: Hurst, 1975), while the best recent work dealing with Aden is Glen Balfour-Paul, *The End of Empire in the Middle East* (Cambridge: Cambridge Univ. Press, 1991). Other major works on the region are British memoirs with the most notable being Tom Hickinbotham, *Aden* (London: Constable, 1958), Kennedy Trevaskis, *Shades of Amber* (London: Hutchinson, 1968), and Charles Johnston, *The View from Steamer Point* (London: Collins, 1964). Tom Little, *South Arabia: Arena of Conflict* (London: Praeger, 1968) and David Ledger, *Shifting Sands* (London: Peninsular Publishing, 1983) remain among the better works written by journalists in Aden during the period.

2. For a detailed examination of Britain's financial situation see Diane Kunz, "British Post-War Sterling Crises" in W. Roger Louis, *Adventures with Britannia* (Austin, 1995), 123–34.

3. Trevaskis, *Shades of Amber*, xii–xiii.

4. Trevaskis, *Shades of Amber*, xiii–xiv.

5. Hickinbotham had spent most of his career in Aden, starting as a member of the Indian Political Service and assistant to the Resident, and later first Governor of Aden, Sir Bernard Reilly. Immediately before his appointment, Hickinbotham had successfully managed the Port Trust of the Colony, supervising the most important economic aspect of the fortress colony. Hickinbotham, *Aden*, 164–170.

6. Hickinbotham to Lyttleton, Secret, 25 October 1952, CO 1015/166.

7. Minutes by Reilly, A. R. Thomas, Marnham and Gorell Barnes, November 1952, CO 1015/166.

8. Minute to Marnham, 9 February 1953, CO 1015/166.

9. Secret, A. D. M. Ross to Marnham, 28 April 1953, CO 1015/166.

10. Secret and Personal letter from E. D. Howe to Marnham, 17 September 1953, CO 1015/166.

11. *The Times*, 8 January 1954.

12. *The Times*, 1 March 1954.

13. *The Times*, 4 April, 1954.

14. Trevaskis, *Shades of Amber*, 45.

15. Secret, Colonial Office Memorandum, "Her Majesty's Government's Long Range Policy in the Aden Protectorate and Aden Colony," 22 September 1955, PREM 11/2616.

16. Hickinbotham kept the federation alive by stating, "The rulers and peoples of these states are entirely free to negotiate among themselves . . . such form of closer association as may suit them best." *The Times*, 2 April 1956. *The Times*, 2 April 1956.

17. *The Times*, 19 May 1956.

18. Norman Brook to Eden, 12 March 1956, PREM 11/2616.

19. Secret, Hickinbotham to Secretary of State for Colonies, 28 April 1956, CO 1015/1202. Emphasis in original.

20. Secret, Secretary of State for Colonies to Hickinbotham, 5 May 1956, CO 1015/1202.

21. Secret Letter from Lord Lloyd to Colonial Office, 8 June 1956, PREM 11/2616.

22. Luce's previous experience had been in the Sudan where he had entered the Sudan Political Service in 1930. Most recently, Luce held the position of the advisor on constitutional and external affairs to the governor-general in the Sudan.

23. In May 1956 during a period of internal strife in the colony, the governor, then Sir Tom Hickinbotham, believed that if more troops were needed in the colony, "a good plan for reinforcement of the Middle East already exists." Little did he know, as the Colonial Office did, that such a plan did not exist. Secret, Hickinbotham to Secretary of State for Colonies, 12 May 1956, PREM 11/2616.

24. Since a detailed examination of the Suez crisis is beyond this work, see Anthony Eden *Full Circle* (London: Houghton Mifflin, 1960), Hugh Thomas, *The Suez Affair* (London: Weidenfield & Nicolson, 1957), and more recently, Louis and Owen, *Suez 1956* (New York: Oxford Univ. Press, 1989) and Keith Kyle, *Suez* (New York: St. Martins, 1991).

25. *Parliamentary Papers* (Commons), *1956–57*, vol. xxiii, Cmnd. 124, Defence: Outline of Future Policy; 1956–1957, 4.

26. *Parliamentary Papers* (Commons), *1956–57*, vol. xxiii, Cmnd. 124, Defence: Outline of Future Policy; 1956–1957, 4.

27. Secret, Luce to Secretary of State for Colonies, 18 June 1957, CO 1015/2066.

28. J. C. Morgan to W. L. Gorell Barnes, 20 June 1957, CO 1015/2066. Emphasis in the original.

29. The change in direction "disappointed" Trevaskis who felt that abandoning federation would result in the "collapse of our fragile colonial stronghold." Even with his dissatisfaction over the change he "could not dispute [Luce's] logic . . . [that] [w]e had flogged the dead horse of federation long enough." Trevaskis, *Shades of Amber*, 127.

30. Secret, Roger Makins to Sir John Macpherson, 8 July 1957, CO 1015/2066.

31. Luce wanted the money to come from the Commonwealth Development and Welfare fund, but at least one Colonial official, advocated "pushing forward with the bolder, or more 'dramatic' approach of trying to persuade

the Treasury." This argument rested on the belief that if they did not pay the money in 1957, "they [the Treasury Office] will in the end have to spend a great deal more on forces, and probably have to spend the money on development as well!" J. C. Morgan to W. L. Gorell Barnes, 20 June 1957, CO 1015/2066.

32. Secret, Roger Makins to Sir John Macpherson, 8 July 1957, CO 1015/2066.

33. Luce to J. C. Morgan, 15 November 1957, CO 1015/2066.

34. Comment by Harold Macmillan on memorandum from P. De Zulueta, 27 December 1957, PREM 11/2616.

35. Secret, Memorandum on Aden Protectorate Policy, 1 January 1958, CO 1015/2067.

36. Trevaskis, *Shades of Amber*, 129.

37. *The Times*, 17 January 1958. Hereafter, the United Arab Republic will be referred to as the UAR.

38. Luce to Gorell Barnes, Top Secret, 27 March 1958, CO 1015/1911.

39. Luce to Gorell Barnes, Top Secret, 28 March 1958, CO 1015/1911.

40. Trevaskis, *Shades of Amber*, 100.

41. *The Times*, 19 April 1958.

42. One squadron of armored cars generally included eight vehicles. In addition, at the time the military presence in Aden consisted of two infantry battalions, the Cameronians, and The Queen's Own Cameron Highlanders. Although this may seem a relatively small addition, it shows the inadequacy of Britain's previous policy in controlling unrest: the use of air policing. For information on air policing see David Omissi, *Air Power and Colonial Control* (Manchester: Manchester Univ. Press, 1990).

43. *The Times*, 17 April 1958.

44. Luce to Gorell Barnes, Top Secret, 27 March 1958, CO 1015/1911.

45. Luce to Gorell Barnes, Top Secret, 27 March 1958, CO 1015/1911.

46. The best background on the ATUC remains D. C. Watt, "Labor Relations and Trade Unionism in Aden, 1952–1960," *Middle East Journal*, Vol. 16, Autumn 1962, 443–456.

47. Trevaskis, *Shades of Amber*, 139.

48. Luce to Gorell Barnes, Secret, 19 May 1958, CO 1015/1667.

49. This figure included £70,000 for the purchase of one squadron of armored cars for the national guards and £150,000 for building the federation's capital with the variable costs in initial political grants depending on the number of states in the new federation.

50. Luce to Gorell Barnes, Secret, 19 May 1958, CO 1015/1667.

51. In addition to the five protectorate rulers, the meetings included Alan Lennox-Boyd, the Earl of Perth (Minister of State for Colonial Affairs), Sir William Luce, W. L. Gorell Barnes, J. C. Morgan, Sir Bernard Reilly, A. J. McIntosh (Asst. Chief Secretary in Aden), and R. R. Johnson (deputy resident advisor and British agent in the protectorate).

52. "Note by the Prime Minister," 28 June 1958, PREM 11/2616.

53. Gorell Barnes to Lennox-Boyd, Secret, 18 June 1958, CO 1015/2124.

54. Lennox-Boyd to Heathcoat Amory, Top Secret, 8 July 1958, CO 1015/2616.

55. Copy of letter, Amory to Lennox-Boyd, 11 July 1958, PREM 11/2616.

56. Lennox-Boyd to Heathcoat Amory, 11 July 1958, PREM 11/2616.

57. Lennox-Boyd to Prime Minister, 13 July 1958, PREM 11/2616.

58. "Notes of a Meeting with Certain Rulers from the Western Aden Protectorate at the Colonial Office at 4.30 P.M. on the 15th July, 1958," Confidential, CO 1015/1667.

59. *The Times*, 11 June 1958.

60. Trevaskis, *Shades of Amber*, p. 129–137. R. J. Gavin declares the decision to support the non-Lahej coalition as the decisive point in British policies toward the area. See *Aden Under British Rule*, 337–338 (particularly, see note 67). But the situation gave the British no options. To the British, support of Sultan Ali meant support of Nasser and a reopening of the wounds of Suez.

61. *The Times*, 11 July 1958.

62. *The Times*, 16 July 1958.

63. Policy paper on Somaliland and Aden, Top Secret, 24 December 1958, CO 1015/1911.

64. *The Times*, 12 February 1959.

65. In 1990 South Yemen and North Yemen unified. The merger placed the political capital at Sana while Aden remained the commercial center for the region with some political autonomy. In 1994 a civil war erupted over perceived inequities of the merger. The Southern forces were quickly defeated with all effective power shifting to Sana.

# 5

# THE GREAT GAME RESUMED: AFGHANISTAN AND THE DEFENSE OF INDIA, 1919–1939



## Mark Jacobsen



As a seaborne empire, Britain did not have to defend its dependent territories against land invasions, at least not so long as it commanded the seas. Historically, this generalization held true except for India, whose northwest border with Afghanistan was not only restive but vulnerable to Russian pressure exerted through Afghanistan. Twice in the nineteenth century the British took up arms against the Afghans to depose rulers thought excessively sympathetic to the Russians, and at all times the British kept a wary eye on Russian intrigues, real or imagined, in Central Asia. This twilight struggle was the "Great Game," prodigiously studied and still capable of generating a fine history. But its twentieth-century aspects remain substantially unstudied.

Fifty years before Russian tanks rolled into Kabul, the defense of Afghanistan against Russian attack was a likely contingency and one made more important with the advent of Bolshevism. Twice in the interwar years, the question assumed an especially acute form, once in 1926–1927 and again in 1931–1933. This chapter surveys these two war scares in the context both of imperial policy toward a former client state and against a major regional rival, resurgent after its collapse in 1917–1921.

That Russia might threaten India by absorbing Afghanistan had worried the British in India since the early nineteenth century. Russia's expansion eastward and her subjugation of the Khanates in Central Asia in the 1860s and 1870s had convinced British authorities that the warlike but politically unorganized tribes of Afghanistan and the Northwest Frontier no longer constituted an effective barrier against any Russian advance to the frontiers of the Indian Empire.

Whether or not the Russians would ever use their position astride India's borders to invade it was beside the point. Simply, the presence of a European state would impose financial and military burdens which Britain could never afford. Moreover, a Russian presence would weaken British prestige within India, weakening British rule even without the inevitable subversion. Thus, Afghanistan had to be preserved as a buffer state, even if it meant war. Since the Second Afghan War of 1878–1880, British policy had been to preserve Afghanistan as an independent buffer state between India and Russia. In 1885 war almost resulted when Russian forces defeated Afghan troops at the Penjdeh oasis near Herat and sliced off a sliver of Afghan territory. Thereafter, the threat had receded, disappearing after the Anglo-Russian entente of 1907.

## URTA TAGAI AND THE DEFENSE OF INDIA

In the late 1920s an apparent Russian threat to invade Afghanistan over a 140-square-mile island occasioned a little-known war scare. Late in 1925 and through the first months of 1926, it appeared that a brief Russian occupation of the island of Urta Tagai in the Amu Darya River [better known to western readers as the Oxus] might presage a Russian invasion of Afghanistan. For the British in Whitehall and in Delhi, the crisis inspired a thoroughgoing reappraisal of Soviet aims and of British strategy in a region where Britain's military resources were as slender as her security interests were great.

The facts were both simple and opaque. In December 1925 a Russian column had crossed the Amu Darya and occupied the large island of Urta Tagai around which the river flowed. The island had been used by Basmachi rebels as a base for raids into Soviet Turkistan, so the Russians' hot pursuit could at least be understood if not condoned.

From the Afghan capital of Kabul came noises of war, although the season of the year precluded either Afghanistan or Russia from deploying substantial forces. Neither could the British employ their own numbers. Tension remained high for two months until the Soviets indicated their willingness to negotiate. The Soviets evacuated the island, and Afghan troops reoccupied it pending the outcome of the mixed Soviet-Afghan commission (three commissioners from each side).[1] Although the willingness of the Soviets to negotiate was a good sign, British strategists were only too aware that negotiations might deadlock and the Afghans then attack the Russians—a conflict the Afghans could hardly hope to win.

The repercussions of the Urta Tagai affair extended well beyond remote Central Asia, for it raised questions of what form the Soviet threat took, of how Britain could deal with it, and of how Britain could defend her Indian interests. Soviet intentions were inscrutable to the British, for the USSR was both a great power and a subversive influence. As a nation, it continued to emulate Tsarist policies in Central Asia that menaced Afghanistan. As the headquarters of the Communist International, the USSR challenged British rule in India. In Central Asia, the Bolsheviks had cleverly harnessed their ideology to reassert Russian control over the Central Asian regimes that sprang up when Tsarist rule collapsed in 1917. By posing as supporters of such indigenous nationalists as the "Young Bokharans" who overthrew the last emir of Bokhara in 1920, the Bolsheviks had demonstrated the essential continuity of Russian foreign policy. Then, too, there was the ideological dimension. The doctrines of Marx and Lenin may have meant little to the average Asian, less to pious Muslims, but the cry to loot the bazaars and to dispossess the landlord appealed to far more basic instincts. In the troubled days of 1920 it had seemed that, as Chief of the General Staff in India, General Sir Claud Jacob put it:

> The whole Middle East is being kept in turmoil in set purpose and on a definite plan . . . the Soviet's declared intention of crippling the British Empire through India. . . . It may safely be asserted that there is hardly a single movement of an anti-British nature in Turkey, Syria, Palestine, Arabia, Mesopotamia, Persia or Afghanistan that they have not sought directly or indirectly to encourage for their own ends, which consist in the destruction of British prestige in Asia and the consolidation of their position on the borders of India, so that they may finally be able to create a revolution in this country.[2]

Another possibility, which hitherto had seemed to be established Russian practice, was that the Soviets aimed to subvert the Afghan government under the guise of development assistance. In 1921 the Russians had signed a friendly treaty with the Afghans that renounced privileges extorted by Imperial Russia, and from 1924 onwards they provided various forms of technical assistance, constructing telegraph lines and roads and managing an air service from Termez to Kabul. In British eyes, both these projects could facilitate any Soviet invasion. Most ominously, they had provided an air mission to Kabul for the infant Afghan Air Force, and Afghan pilots had trained at Tashkent.

On the face of it, the Soviet occupation of Urta Tagai ran completely counter to established Soviet policy, suggesting two additional possibilities, neither very appetizing: that the Soviets sought an occasion to invade and occupy Afghanistan outright, or that they aimed merely to encourage the Afghan provinces north of the Hindu Kush to rise against the government in Kabul. The inhabitants of the northern third of Afghanistan were Tajiks, Uzbegs, and Turkomans, ethnic groups more akin to tribesmen in Soviet Russia than to the Durani and Ghilzai tribes ruling Afghanistan. Many observers believed that the Russians had established the pseudo-republics of Turkmenistan, Uzbekia, and Tajikistan precisely to sow divisions among citizens' kin in Afghanistan and Persia and to create the unsettled conditions that could serve as a pretext for a Soviet takeover.[3] Whatever the case, the British knew how easily the Soviets might manipulate the nationalities of Central Asia, and they feared the consequences if the overly confident Afghans tried their luck against the Red Army.

In Whitehall, the Chiefs of Staff defined the issue starkly enough. India's security depended upon her not sharing a common frontier with Russia and upon Afghanistan's remaining a buffer state, strategically neutered by her lack of railroads and decent highways. Should the Soviets annex Afghan Turkistan, that is, Afghanistan north of the Hindu Kush, the Hindu Kush would become de facto India's northwest frontier and Soviet Russia India's neighbor: "A common frontier with Russia would be a canker for ever eating into the resources of the Empire." And of Russia's aims there was no doubt:

> The available evidence leads us to believe that the present policy of Soviet Russia towards India is identical with that adopted in the past by Imperial Russia. The methods of the Soviet are, however, more insidious, more intangible, and, therefore, in the ultimate issue, more dangerous than those employed by their predecessors in the past.[4]

In Whitehall the Conservative government headed by Stanley Baldwin established a strong Defence of India subcommittee to the Committee of Imperial Defence (CID). The Defence of India committee met nine times in the spring of 1927. Because its deliberations took place well after the immediate crisis, the Defence of India committee was able to conduct a sustained examination of the entire question, the only such evaluation during the interwar period. Chaired by the India secretary, Lord Birkenhead, its members were Winston Churchill, Chancellor of the Exchequer; Lord Peel, former India Secretary and party grandee who held office as Commissioner of Works; Sir Samuel Hoare, Air Secretary; Sir Austen Chamberlain, Foreign Secretary; and Leo Amery, Colonial Secretary.[5] Prime Minister Stanley Baldwin himself sat in from time to time, and the committee took evidence from India Office officials; the former Viceroy, Lord Reading; and from such military luminaries as Chief of the Air Staff, Sir Hugh Trenchard; Chief of the Imperial General Staff (CIGS), Field-Marshal Sir George Milne; and Field-Marshal Earl Haig, himself former Chief of the General Staff in India. The great issue before the Birkenhead committee was whether the Russians would seize the northern third of Afghanistan and if so what Britain's proper response should or could be. The answers were not reassuring. A spokesman for the War Office had told the Chiefs of Staff that war with Russia was "more than likely to take place within the next ten years."[6] Both Birkenhead and Churchill agreed with this assessment.

As much as the military believed that invasion represented the greatest danger to Afghanistan, the political spokesmen of the Indian Empire emphasized the political dangers of subversion from within. The analysis developed by the Indian Foreign and Political Department held that Afghanistan's foreign policy aimed to balance Britain against Russia, leaning toward one to the extent that the other threatened. Paradoxically, therefore, it was in Britain's hands whether Afghanistan drifted into Soviet arms. Viceroy Lord Irwin noted that the Soviets had established their influence with the Afghans after the First World War by abrogating their 1907 unequal treaty with Afghanistan at the same time the British were struggling to maintain control of Afghanistan's foreign relations. Likewise, the Soviets had been able to foster Afghanistan's air force precisely because the British had bombed Kabul during the brief Third Afghan War in 1919.[7] From these observations, Irwin went on to a more controversial recommendation. In view of its fragmented tribal character, Afghanistan might be better off shorn of its lands north of the Hindu Kush and maybe even the Herat district in its northwest plains. The Hazaras were Mongolians, Shiite and very opposed to Afghan rule, and the Turkomens, Uzbeks, and Tajiks dwelling there hardly belonged under Afghan rule. Birkenhead adduced a different reason to steer clear of King Amanullah. Amanullah had come to power in suspicious circumstances in 1919, after the murder of his pro-British father. He had promptly declared war on Britain, fought a brief Third Afghan War, and then proceeded to stir up the frontier tribes in hopes of extorting a subsidy from the British. Throughout his early years, Amanullah had coquetted with the Bolsheviks, even while entertaining grandiose visions of a Central Asian confederacy under Afghan suzerainty. Such an unstable ruler, as prone to flirt with the Soviets as to fight them, could not be given any guarantees involving British prestige. A trivial incident could draw Britain into war.[8] As the Minister at Kabul, Sir Francis Humphrys, explained, "There is a gap of nearly 1,500 miles in our intelligence between Kashgar [in Sinkiang] and Meshed [northeast Persia]," and in place of reliable information Britain depended on local accounts from a country, "where truth and report are habitually divorced."[9]

Behind the question whether Britain *should* defend Afghanistan lay the very pragmatic concern whether either the Afghans or the British *could*. The Indian General Staff questioned the competency of both the Afghan army to defend its borders and that of the Indian Army to rescue Afghanistan. Of the Afghan army, the Indian General Staff had reported in 1925 that "training is almost entirely confined to the parade ground, musketry is almost unheard of and field training is very elementary." Afghan artillery was primitive, shells having percussion fuses since few gunners could set timed fuses.[10] Two years later the Defence of India Committee echoed this warning, agreeing that the Afghan Army was:

> . . . not a fighting machine in any proper modern use of the term. It is true that it possesses modern rifles, machine guns and breech-loading artillery; but the attempt which has been made to organise it on a European model has so far succeeded only in destroying a part of the fighting value which it might have possessed had it remained on an irregular, tribal basis.[11]

Ethnic factors complicated the picture. Because the Afghan Army was drawn from Pashtu-speaking peoples east of the Hindu Kush, its reliability north of the Hindu Kush was questionable. If the Afghans could not defend their homeland, the somber truth was that neither could the British. Afghanistan had no railroads and few paved roads. Because a Russian invader could concentrate in secrecy at the railhead of Termez opposite Mazar-i-Sherif, the Russians could be in Kabul within a matter of days. Unfortunately, the state of Indian Army transport would not allow an effective and timely counterthrust from India. As early as 1907, it had been calculated that war with Russia in Afghanistan would require three million camels.[12] Even so brief a campaign as that of June 1919 had compelled the Indian military to mobilize 450,000 camels, horses, and mules, despite some motor transport having been available.[13]

Seven years later, the Indian General Staff reckoned that only 22,000 horses and mules would have to be found, but even this figure exceeded Indian resources. Motorized transport was little better, for postwar economizing had retarded purchases of trucks. The army estimated that it needed almost 1,400 additional trucks before it could mobilize to plan. India had no tanks apart from some experimental models. Signals, reported the General Staff, were "most unsatisfactory." The army lacked British officers. Moreover, "large numbers of technical personnel will be required [from Britain] on mobilisation and at present no means of obtaining them exists."[14]

Because of these shortcomings, only two divisions of the Field Army—nominally four divisions strong—could mobilize on schedule. Thus, although the Indian Army was a fine force on paper, it lacked the administrative and supply units to sustain a campaign of more than frontier dimensions. A war fought on the frontiers of India with a major European land power was precisely what had to be avoided, for it was a war the Indian Army could not win. Even the more modest project of defending the southern two-thirds of Afghanistan was a logistical nightmare. If Afghan Turkistan were written off, the Indian General Staff calculated that seven divisions would still be needed to hold the Hindu Kush line and Kabul with it. To hold the southern line, that is, the approaches to Kandahar, required an additional four divisions and three cavalry brigades, the equivalent of the entire British and Indian armies. Successfully prosecuting this war meant building railroads into Afghanistan and adding three new divisions to the Indian field army as well as a major reequipment program for both the army and the RAF in India. And these calculations assumed the 'Afghan army fighting alongside the British and a swarm of tribesmen harassing the Soviets' ever-lengthening lines of communication.[15]

The geography of Afghanistan also supported the appraisal by the Indian military. The most defensible position in northern Afghanistan was the line of the Hindu Kush/Koh-i-Baba mountains, all but one or two of whose passes were closed half the year by snow. These two passes converged on the capital and largest city, Kabul, which also could be reached by road from India fairly easily. If the Soviets crossed the border, the Khyber Railway could be pushed through, a step vastly simplifying the logistics of such a campaign. A comparatively modest number of troops could hold Kabul, and the RAF could be used to great effect in the key passes. In the arid south, the potential lines of advance were limited to four, each following the course of a river or seasonal stream. Of the four routes, that of the Helmand River offered the best water and best existing communications with Kabul and with Kandahar, Afghanistan's second largest city, and one easily linked by rail to India. Its only disadvantage as a defensive position was its distance from the Soviet border, which meant surrendering much territory but which extended the Soviets' lines of communication and compelled them to advance through desolate country where lack of water severely limited an invader's size and movements. Here lay the crux. Britain could not realistically hope to project Indian military strength into northern Afghanistan (or anywhere else threatening Russia), but not to do so weakened India, perhaps irretrievably, and threw into question both the prestige of Britain and the worth of British commitments elsewhere. To allow Afghan Turkistan to slip into the Soviet orbit either directly or as a sort of protectorate such as Outer Mongolia, would weaken British rule on the Northwest Frontier, within India, and, ultimately, throughout the Empire.

This bleak analysis with its implicit recommendations of political accommodation did not sit well with every quarter. At the time the committee sat, the military secretary of the India Office, normally a secondary staff officer, was a far more formidable figure, Field-Marshal Sir Claud Jacob, Indian CGS between 1918–1925 and interim commander-in-chief in 1925. The product of a longtime Anglo-Indian family and a descendant of the nineteenth-century frontier paladin John Jacob of Jacobabad, Jacob subscribed to the view that for India to show any weakness in the face of a challenge was to throw away the very cement of the Indian Empire—prestige. In his view, neither Afghanistan nor India was a nation-state in the European sense; rather, they were conglomerations of peoples held together by superior political organization. Bolshevism threatened Afghanistan just as nationalism threatened India, and to give ground in one theater was to give ground in the other.[16]

In a series of papers and in oral testimony, Jacob attacked the Indian government and General Staff's views, and rallied his Whitehall colleagues to take a far stiffer line. If Russia were permitted to occupy the north of Afghanistan, the Afghan state would disintegrate and tribal chaos ensue. Persia would fall victim to Soviet-inspired subversion, which would expose British Baluchistan to penetration as well. This disorder would spill over into India's Northwest Frontier Province. Jacob found support from the CIGS, Field-Marshal Sir George Milne, who fully shared Jacob's political interpretation, recalling Lenin's adage that the "road to London goes through Delhi" to caution that "it does not seem impossible that Russian political strategy may be aiming at securing political domination over Afghanistan, with the object of developing it as a defensive buffer, to be consolidated and exploited as a jumping-off place for the next move towards India."[17] Moreover, whatever the intentions of Russia the implications for British rule in India were even greater: "We can defeat an enemy, more especially an Oriental one, only in one way, and that is by attacking him . . . what is really at stake is the integrity of the British Empire, and surely, no effort is too great to ensure this."

This approach meant that the whole weight of the British Expeditionary Force (BEF) would have to be thrown into the scales against Russia in a region where BEF's armor and mobility would pay handsome dividends. The result was the "Defence of India Plan" approved by the Committee of Imperial Defence in June 1928. Milne and the military planners of the Imperial General Staff envisaged the Soviets making a two-pronged thrust: a slow infantry advance through the Hindu Kush toward Kabul, which could be halted by two infantry divisions of the Indian field army assisted by the RAF's developing air bases at Kabul, and an armored thrust along the line Kandahar-Farah-Herat, which would be blocked by a division and a cavalry brigade from India advancing ahead of the British Expeditionary Force from home. Having boldly seized the principal political prizes of Afghanistan, the British would extend existing railroads to Kabul and Kandahar to support a major campaign involving nineteen divisions.[18]

To the Indian General Staff, this whole project was the height of unreality. Staff planners at Delhi discounted the possibility of active Soviet intervention and planned instead for what they viewed as the most probable contingency, a war with Afghanistan and concomitant tribal risings. From an Indian point of view, British forces had no choice but to fight on the strategic defensive. The Indian plan envisaged a forward defense in the Hindu Kush mountains, not at the Afghan northern frontier on the Oxus. The General Staff in India reasoned that if it tried to defend the territorial integrity of Afghanistan, Indian forces would be fighting close to Russian lines of communication and bases and correspondingly far from their own bases. The passes over the Hindu Kush through which British forces would be supplied were snowbound five months of the year, hardly favorable conditions. Were Britain to take the fight to the Russians, the Soviets would defend a land frontier with a vastly superior army. To adopt a strategy that would end India's strategic isolation would precipitate dangers that otherwise were only conjectural.[19]

The extant Indian plan of campaign for a war in Afghanistan, really a war *with* Afghanistan, was termed the "Blue Plan," and Jacob was quite familiar with it. The Blue Plan envisaged a two-pronged advance into Afghanistan, in the north a rapid advance on Jalalabad in the Khyber Pass preceded by an "intensive air offensive" that would continue on to Kabul. In the south, mobile British forces based at Quetta would take Kandahar, the second most important city in the kingdom. Because of the difficulties of supplying an advance that still depended on animal transport moving slowly through hostile and barren country, both plans envisaged Indian Army engineers building broad-gauge rail lines through Afghan territory to both Kabul and Kandahar.[20]

This appraisal derived from the Third Afghan War of 1919. Although lacking in the heroics of the two earlier Afghan wars, the ten-day war of May and June 1919 profoundly affected the British in India. The war itself was no great thing: the Afghans advanced a few miles into the Khyber and Kurram Passes. When British troops shortly went over to the offensive, the Afghan advance collapsed. But 1919 went on to become the true *annus horriblis* of twentieth-century India, for the Afghan attack suspiciously had followed all too swiftly after widespread violence in the Punjab. The Afghan War then inspired tribal risings that took the better part of four years to stamp out. A repetition of these events, which cost the Indian Army sorely in lives and money, had to be avoided.

As a result, the Indian plan, bound in blue covers, only superficially resembled the War Office Defence of India plan in envisaging a two-pronged advance on Afghanistan. In all important respects, it was a different plan, since it limited the advance, assumed a different lineup of forces, and discounted entirely the possibility that the British Expeditionary Force from home might join the Indian Army.[21]

Because some resemblance existed in the two plans' early stages, the issue of which plan was definitive was never resolved. As the Afghans and the Soviets had patched up their differences while the Defence of India Committee deliberated, the whole question was consigned to the file cabinets. By the early 1930s, scant progress had been made in the modernization needed to effect either plan. When the full force of the financial blizzard struck India and England alike in 1931, the Indian General Staff realized it would not have the motor transport units specified under the Blue Plan any time soon. Without motor transport, an advance to Kabul required an unacceptably large amount of animal transport and infantry necessary to safeguard these tempting targets. The army in India found itself facing the classic dilemma of unmechanized armies in difficult country. To feed the troops, such armies had to carry prodigious quantities of supplies. Such transport required large numbers of animals, each in turn requiring its own fodder, which in turn meant more transport. These requirements had an exponential effect on the numbers of animals needed for an entire campaign. The whole lot moved ponderously, requiring ever-larger lines of communications troops, all of which required yet greater supplies and transportation of their own. Short of massive railroad construction, the only way out of this vicious circle was to scale back the offensive.

Accordingly, the Indian General Staff produced in the fall of 1931 a new plan, bound in pink covers and known inevitably as the "Pink Plan," which offered only a limited advance on Jalalabad in the north, while still pursuing the southern route deep into Afghanistan to Kandahar. As ever with plans drawn up in India, the Pink Plan focused on Afghanistan and the tribes, and the weight of the army's manpower was to be concentrated on its lines of communication, where the troops on the two lines of advance would keep the tribes at a respectful distance.[22]

The War office approved but reluctantly, criticizing the Indian Army's decision not to occupy Kabul while acknowledging that the Indian Army's readiness had been sapped by fiscal retrenchment and by Indianization—the progressive replacement of junior British officers by Indians for the Dominion army promised India. Still, the War Office questioned whether merely occupying Jalalabad would bring the Afghans to sue for peace. The Pink Plan provided for this possibility by positing a second phase that involved the BEF's being shipped out from home. Not that the War Office relished this prospect. By now, the expansive mood of 1927 had clearly evaporated. The Imperial General Staff, in phrases that were to be heard again in the decade to come, warned against "any action which tends to increase the liabilities of the Imperial forces at a time when this country would find it extremely difficult to provide for any increase in its commitments."[23] But because the Pink Plan resembled the first phases of the Defence of India Plan, their discrepancies were again overlooked. By this time, however, the political assumption underlying the Pink Plan—that Afghanistan itself was a likely enemy—no longer held good. Afghan traditionalists, alarmed by King Amanullah's quixotic efforts at modernization, had overthrown him in 1929. So departed an individual whom the Defence of India Plan had succinctly characterized as "an unbalanced and unscrupulous barbarian."[24] His successor, Nadir Shah, had commanded the Afghan army in 1919, and despite this experience, or perhaps because of it, he proved a good friend of the British. As the secretary of the India Office's Political and Secret Department noted with evident satisfaction in 1931, "The repetition of any such obvious folly as the Third Afghan War is consequently most improbable."[25]

## NADIR SHAH: ASSET AND LIABILITY

Nadir plainly mistrusted the Soviets, and during his reign Soviet-Afghan relations perceptibly cooled. Russian troops actually crossed the Oxus again in July 1930 in hot pursuit of Ibrahim Beg, leader of a Basmachi band that had long eluded the Red Army, and their diplomatic pressure led Nadir to disperse the band. That sort of pressure, combined with heavy Russian hints to accept Russian economic and development aid, led Nadir in early 1931 to seek assurances of British support in the event of conflict with Russia. The reply given on that occasion was that Britain could not be indifferent to unprovoked aggression against Afghanistan but that the exact response would depend on circumstances. About a year later, the Afghan prime minister and foreign minister repeated the query, this time drawing attention to diplomatic pressure from Moscow to permit a Russian air service between Termez and Kabul and to conclude a trade treaty favorable to the Soviets. One of its terms would be extraterritorial privileges for Russian officials and trading establishments. With some urgency, the Afghans repeated their request of a year earlier to know the British attitude about Soviet diplomatic pressure. They also inquired about the probability of Soviet aggression. This time, after prolonged official debate in Delhi and in Whitehall, the ambassador at Kabul replied more forcefully that Britain would regard an unprovoked Russian attack on Afghanistan as an attack on British and Indian interests, indeed an attack that would force Britain to respond as if her own interests were seriously threatened. In the context of 1932, however, these assurances meant diplomacy and economic pressure. Promise of a diplomatic rupture and economic sanctions were the furthest the ambassador was prepared to go.[26]

Although a welcome change from Amanullah's past flirtations with the Soviets, Nadir's request for help was met with the bland reply that Britain would not be indifferent to Afghanistan's interests. He returned with the same query a year later. The Foreign Secretary, Sir John Simon, allowed that if the Soviets threatened Afghanistan's integrity without provocation, Britain would intervene diplomatically and even commercially, a consequential step in the Foreign Office view, as the Five-Year Plan depended heavily on Britain's accepting Russian exports. Otherwise, Simon bleakly advised, the Afghans could join the League of Nations.[27]

The Foreign Office questioned whether the Soviets had either the inclination or the capacity to invade Afghanistan. Japanese pressure in Manchuria, as well as the commitment to the Five-Year Plan, suggested that the Soviets would avoid foreign adventures, especially in so unpropitious a locale as Afghanistan. Ultimately, Russia threatened India, and this threat was political, not military. For this reason the Foreign Office doubted whether Russia would attack an independent Muslim state. To do so would undermine their ongoing subversion within India.[28] This confidence proved misplaced as Soviet-Afghan relations deteriorated throughout 1933. The Afghans were troubled by Soviet railroad building north of the Amu Darya and suspected the Russians' eagerness to build or extend all-weather roads linking Kabul with the Soviet Union. Moreover, the Russians wanted to bridge the Amu Darya and to extend their railroads to tie up with the Kabul highway. These forceful representations led to an Afghan request for British military advice on defending this highway, a query the Government of India interpreted as foreshadowing a request for full-scale staff talks. The home government, too, saw this and took it as evidence of dissatisfaction with previous British assurances, if such they could be characterized.

Most seriously, on 8 November 1933, King Nadir Shah fell to an assassin's bullets while reviewing a school in Kabul. Much to the relief of the British, his son, Zahir Shah, succeeded to the throne without any substantial move to restore the deposed King Amanullah, whose presence was sure to have been an irritant to British flesh. No evidence appeared to link the assassination with the Russians; the son of a political rival executed by Nadir did him in without benefit of outside assistance. In the wake of Nadir's murder, however, the question of British interests appeared in a more somber light than before.

Both the Indian and the British military favored taking active steps to demonstrate support for the Afghans and to enhance their ability to defend themselves. Whatever their intentions might be, the Soviets now had the capacity to invade Afghanistan and seize Kabul well before the British could respond. A troubled Government of India compared recent Russian extensions of their railways to the pre-1914 German construction pointing at Belgium. Similarly, road construction linking Kabul with Termez in Soviet Turkistan across the Oxus facilitated a swift motorized Russian coup aimed at the Afghan capital. At any rate, the Russians could more readily advance from Termez to the crest of the Hindu Kush Mountains than the British could advance from their railhead in the Khyber Pass.[29] The military secretary at the India Office, Lieutenant-General Sir John Coleridge, again raised the specter of the Soviets' supporting some kind of revolt in Afghan Turkistan in order to weaken the government in Kabul. Their aim, he believed, was to "Sovietize" Afghanistan, inflaming opinion against Britain, so that a subsequent invasion of India would pass through friendly territory.[30]

The Soviets had begun to rearm by 1934. The Chiefs of Staff knew they had made "notable advances" in chemical warfare, which they would use on the ground and from the air. They had doubled their air force since 1928, and all their modern airplanes could reach the Indus, while their heavy bombers had sufficient radius to reach Lahore. They had made "remarkable progress" in armored warfare, moving from 150 tanks in 1931 to nearly 2,400 two years later. Whereas the feared armored thrust through the Afghan desert to Kandahar had been a fantasy in 1926, the prospect of a Russia *coup de main* against Kabul by a specially organized armored and infantry force was eminently feasible eight years later.[31]

This, however, was the most the Soviets could hope to achieve. Neither the Indian nor the Whitehall military believed the Russians could sustain a campaign in Central Asia. Whatever its paper strength, the Red Army suffered from the basic limitations of Soviet society: lack of skilled labor, undeveloped chemicals and explosives industries, poor railways, and unreliable personnel. In the unguarded words of the Chiefs of Staff, " . . . the Russian people are improvident, unreliable and lacking in organizing ability . . . " Indeed, the Chiefs of Staff saw the renascent Red Army as inferior to its tsarist predecessor, and rated the current Russian threat to India below that of the nineteenth century. The same went for the Red air force:

> . . . it is difficult to believe that the Russians, who, both before and during the war, proved themselves the least capable of European nations to exploit scientific inventions, should have been transformed in 17 years of revolution to a people who will lead the world in aviation for the purpose of aggression.[32]

Across Whitehall, Coleridge concurred, "We beat the Germans, why not the Russians? The Great War proved, and the Afghans know it, that one German is equal to four Russians."[33] Whatever the military ratio of nationalities, Russian tanks and aircraft were inferior to comparable British types, and Soviet military aviation and armor suffered from teething troubles unlikely to be rapidly overcome. On balance, concluded an Indian General Staff appraisal, "The quality of the Red Army is below that of a first-class European power and definitely inferior to the combined British and Indian forces."[34] One wonders if the authors of these sentiments later had reason to reconsider their judgments.

More to the point, the Soviets, whatever their ham-handed diplomacy with Kabul, were unlikely to invade Afghanistan in the midst of their five-year plan and in the face of a resurgent Japanese presence on the Asian mainland. Thus fortified, the Cabinet decided to instruct the British ambassador at Kabul to offer military consultations on possible improvements to the road linking Kabul with northern Afghanistan *if* the Afghans raised the issue. There were several good reasons to proceed with circumspection. As much as Nadir's death stemmed from a blood feud between families, it also suggested that any Afghan ruler widely criticized as subservient to the British (as Nadir had been for distancing himself from the widespread frontier disturbances of 1930–1931) might put himself at risk. Above all, any British actions that might suggest the Afghan rulers were acting at Britain's behest had to be avoided.

As events unfolded in 1934, the Afghans let the matter drop. The Soviets certainly retreated from their earlier attitude. Evidently, British willingness to entertain such projects satisfied the Afghans, so the Cabinet never had to decide whether to guarantee the Afghan border. Nonetheless, the Soviet bogey took its time dying. Afghan relations with Moscow continued unsettled, and as late as 1935 the Chiefs of Staff warned that a massive Soviet offensive against the entire Middle East was in the cards.[35]

## THE END OF THE GREAT GAME

A year later, as India and Britain alike prepared to rebuild their military, Sir John Coleridge ventured that the focus should no longer be Russia but Italy and Germany. From within the War Office's Directorate of Military Operations, General John Dill cautioned that:

> . . . although the German menace has grown so much greater that it tends to monopolise the spotlight, the Russian danger has grown no less. . . . The furthest we can go is probably to assume that the Russian menace is not imminent partly because they are terrified of Germany in the West and Japan in the East.[36]

By this time, Dill's was a voice from the past. From 1936 onwards, the threats to which Coleridge had drawn attention grew larger, and the defense of Hong Kong, Singapore, Egypt, and Burma came to occupy the Indian General Staff. Once the field army's fourth division was earmarked as External Defence Troops in 1938, only a scratch force of three cavalry brigades and five and a half infantry brigades could be spared to implement the Pink Plan. Of this only one brigade had its full quota of first-line transport, and the remainder would have to wait for theirs for three months after mobilization—if there were no other military needs elsewhere in the Empire. Then, too, the frontier, whose garrisoning had been in large measure intended to secure India's traditional invasion route, continued to give trouble, sucking in the equivalent of five brigades of the field army by 1937, while two brigades were more or less permanently tied down in Baluchistan.

By the decade's end, the Afghan-Soviet bogey was at last recognized for what it had become much earlier—a chimera. General Claude Auchinleck spoke for the progressive Indian Army officer when he wrote that the army in India had been too long handicapped by a

> . . . stereotyped plan of operations against Afghanistan—a plan drawn up with conviction in the years immediately succeeding the Third Afghan War but subsequently retained *faute de mieux* with occasional variations reflecting the outlook of successive governments. The General Staff will be glad to have their hands freed as of recent years this Afghan plan has lacked reality.[37]

Although it may have been better to have planned against an unlikely war than not to have planned at all, the unlikelihood of either the Afghan or the Soviet conflict taking place deprived these exercises of most of their value. It furthered a disinclination by the Indian and the British general staffs to coordinate their efforts, to "think imperially." Most significantly and ironically, the Pink and Blue plans validated the Indian military's preoccupation with frontier campaigning, since a pacified frontier made possible those ambitious parallel thrusts to Kabul and to Kandahar. Yet the forward policy pursued in tribal areas after 1921 proved costly in the demands it made on the Indian military, condemning the army to forego modernization while ensuring that it remained oriented to frontier fighting even in the face of world war. One cannot help thinking that for all the planning and debating that went on, the wisest counsels were those of the diplomats, who knew that the Afghans would be the stoutest defenders of their own soil. As Sir Francis Humphrys put it in 1927:

> If it can be said that in the past Afghanistan used to whirl in England's orbit . . . it may at least be asserted that the time has definitely gone by when this vain, fanatical and unbridled people would ever consent to tie

itself to the chariot wheels of another or to be regarded as the protege of a foreign power. From the King downwards to the camel driver who swaggers through the bazaars of India and Central Asia, the breath in the nostrils of the Afghan is independence.[38]

## REFERENCES


1. The fullest account of the crisis is in Ludwig Adamec, *Afghanistan's Foreign Affairs to the Mid-Twentieth-Century* (Tucson: Univ. of Arizona Press, 1974), 109–11.

2. "The Present Situation in the Middle East and Central Asia," 12 May 1921, IMR 2, CAB 16/38, Public Record Office, London, hereafter PRO.

3. R. M. Hodgson, British chargé, Moscow, to Foreign Office, "Note on Anglo-Afghan Relations," 24 July 1925, FO 418/64, N4553/342/97, PRO.

4. "Afghanistan: Report by the Chiefs of Staff," 12 July 1926, COS 45, CAB 53/12, PRO.

5. Two participants left records of the Defence of India Committee. Lord Imsay, then serving on the Cabinet Secretariat, treated it in his *Memoirs* (London, 1960), pp. 60–1, as did Leo Amery, whose *Diaries*, ed. Julian Amery (London, 1987), lay bare the divisions within the committee, 500–2.

6. Statement by Maj.-Gen. Sir J. R. E. Charles, Director of Military Operations and Intelligence, COS mtg. 47, 27 July 1926, CAB 53/12, PRO.

7. Irwin Despatch 9 (1926), 7 Oct. 1926, Annex A to CID 149-D, CAB 16/83, PRO.

8. Birkenhead memo, "Afghanistan," 17 June 1926, CID 142-D, CAB 6/5, PRO.

9. Humphrys memo, "The Russo-Afghan Frontier," 19 June 1927, DI 21, CAB 16/83, PRO.

10. Gen. Staff, India, *Military Report on Afghanistan*, (Army Headquarters: Simla, 1925), British Library, Oriental and India Office Collections, London (hereafter, OIOC), L/MIL/17/14/5.

11. "Defence of India: First Report of the Sub-Committee," 19 Dec. 1927, CID 158-D, CAB 6/5, PRO.

12. John Gooch, *The Plans of War* (London: Macmillan, 1967), 215, 221–2.

13. Lt.-Gen. G. N. Molesworth, *Afghanistan 1919* (Bombay: Orient Longmans, 1962), vii.

14. Field-Marshal Sir G. N. Milne, CIGS, "State of Preparedness of the Army in India," 4 May 1927, DI 8, CAB 16/83, PRO.

15. "The Integrity of Afghanistan: Its Importance to the Defence of India and the Military Possibilities of Maintaining It against Russian Aggression," n.d. (c. Oct. 1926, encl. to Annex A, CID 149-D, CAB 6/5. The Indian CGS, Gen. Sir Andrew Skeen, discussed the issue before the 5th mtg. of the Birkenhead Committee, 10 May 1927, CAB 16/83, PRO.

16. "Afghanistan," 7 Oct. 1926, Annex C to CID 149-D, CAB 6/5, PRO.

17. "Memorandum by the CIGS on the Integrity of Afghanistan," Annex D to CID 149-D, CAB 6/5, PRO.

18. The Defence of India Plan is outlined in the initial report of the Birkenhead Committee, CID 158-D, 19 Dec. 1927. The Committee discussed it at its third and fourth mtgs., 26 Apr. and 3 May 1927, CAB 16/83, PRO.

19. 'Note on CID papers 140 D, 143 D, 145 D, 147 D, and 148 D' by Maj-Gen. Sir Walter Kirke, offg. CGS, to Viceroy, 5 May 1927, Kirke papers, OIOC, Eur. Mss. E 396/10.

20. The plan is described in detail in Maj.-Gen. Sir Walter Kirke's memo, "New Plan (Blue)" n.d., Kirke Papers, OIOC, Eur. Mss. E 396/10.

21. Bisheshwar Prasad, *Defence of India: Policy and Plans* (Combined Historical Section: New Delhi, 1963), p. 30. The Blue Plan in effect concerned war with Afghanistan; the Pink Plan addressed a war involving Russia.

22. "Plan of Operations: Afghanistan," WO 33/1266, PRO.

23. Untitled War Office paper, 10 Sept. 1931, L/MIL/7/5508, OIOC.

24. CID 158-D, CAB 6/5, PRO.

25. Note by J. C. Walton, 28 July 1931, L/MIL/7/5508, OIOC.

26. The entire process by which these mild reassurances were developed and then communicated can be followed in L/P&S/12/1682, OIOC.

27. Simon despatch to Sir Robert Maconachie, Minister at Kabul, 17 Oct. 1932, encl. to CID 182-D, CAB 6/6, PRO.

28. Foreign Office memo, 15 Sept. 1932, WO 32/3518, PRO.

29. Lord Hailsham, War Secretary, "Policy in Regard to Afghanistan," 8 Feb. 1934, CP 36(34), Appendix II to CID 186-D, and Govt. of India Despatch I (Foreign and Pol. Dept.), 4 Jan. 1934, Appendix III to CID 186-D, CAB 6/6, PRO. Coleridge's appreciation of 8 Feb. 1934, is in P938, L/P&S/12/1683, OIOC.

30. Minute, 4 Dec. 1933, WS/1/299, OIOC.

31. "Afghanistan: British Policy," COS 326, 23 Feb. 1934, CID 185-D, CAB 6/6, PRO.

32. "Afghanistan British Policy."

33. Coleridge min., 8 Feb. 1934, WS/1/299, OIOC.

34. Undated Indian General Staff paper, L/P&S/12/1682, OIOC.

35. "Imperial Defence Policy: Annual Review by the Chiefs of Staff, 1935," 29 Apr. 1935, COS 372, CAB 53/24, PRO.

36. Dill to Coleridge, 26 March 1936, WS/1/180, OIOC.

37. Memo by Brigs. C. J. Auchinleck and Sidney F. Muspratt, n.d. (c. spring 1939), WS/1/155, OIOC.

38. Despatch to Foreign Office, 21 Feb. 1927, encl. 1 to CID 152-D, CAB 16/83, PRO.

# 6

# REDISCOVERING THE GREAT GAME: SIR OLAF CAROE, THE COLD WAR, AND THE PACIFIC CENTURY

## Peter John Brobst

"Forms change," Sir Olaf Caroe wrote in 1955, "but there is a reality which remains. In terms of international politics today the reality is that, as once in the nineteenth century in Asia, there are now in the whole world two major concentrations of power, one continental, and the other a string of like-thinking nations linked by the sea."[1] The former official of the Raj had rediscovered the Great Game, the Victorian contest for mastery of Asia, in the Cold War. As foreign secretary to the British government of India throughout the Second World War, Caroe had devoted much time and energy to speculation about the strategic future of the British Empire. Although he clearly appreciated the obvious point that postwar decolonization, combined with the advent of air power, portended momentous change, Caroe emphasized continuities between past and present. He believed that the Great Game represented a remarkably resilient frame of reference in which to make sense of the Asian situation amid shifting ideologies and power balances. Caroe's thought not only offers a compelling perspective on the Cold War, but may also help observers of the post-Soviet scene to rediscover the Great Game for themselves in the notion of a coming "Pacific Century."

To suggest this is not to be nostalgic. There is a tendency in the postcolonial, American-led west to consign South Asia to the "periphery" of world power. A recent study of American policy toward India and Pakistan is typical. The author concludes that as the result of an exaggerated estimate of the Communist danger, "the United States deliberately extended the Cold War into South Asia. . . . "[2] This vantage is too narrow. From it, the Cold War appears as though it occurred in a historical vacuum; the traditional centrality of South Asia in the global balance is lost; and South Asians falsely seem passive and inward looking. The prevalence of such perspectives has contributed to repeated surprises: surprise in 1979 that the major Soviet land-grab of the Cold War occurred in South Asia, and surprise more recently with India's decision to carry out nuclear weapons tests.

This chapter proposes that the imperial vision of the Great Game offers a useful corrective. The argument is that students wishing to comprehend modern international politics should keep South Asia front and center, despite Washington's traditional treatment of the region as the eastern appendage to the State Department's Near Eastern subsection and the western extremity of the Pentagon's Pacific Command. As Olaf Caroe admonished in 1945, South Asia must not "be conceived as situated on the fringe of a Pacific system, thus following a vision which is natural to Americans, but as a central constellation from which others in the Indian Ocean in the long run are likely to radiate."[3] In fact, it was Caroe who put forward perhaps the most eloquent, certainly the most comprehensive, explanation of the Great Game as an enduring model of Asian geopolitics.

Strategist, proconsul, pamphleteer, Caroe was an archetypal master of the Great Game. He came from the upper-middle class background common among British administrators who served in India. Although of Danish ancestry, he was born and grew up in Surrey around 1900. His father was William Caroe, the well-known ecclesiastical architect. Caroe attended Winchester before matriculating in Magdalen College, Oxford, where he read Classics. He originally went to India during the First World War as an officer in Britain's territorial army. In 1919, he returned to India with an appointment to the Indian Civil Service. He soon won a coveted transfer to the Indian Political Service, the elite arm of British rule charged with monitoring the great princely states as well as India's borderlands. During the 1920s and 1930s, Caroe served in a variety of posts, including assignments to Peshawar, to Quetta, to Delhi as deputy foreign secretary, and to the Persian Gulf as acting resident. He was foreign secretary to the government of India throughout the Second World War and afterward was Britain's last governor on India's North-West Frontier, the gateway between Central Asia and the subcontinent. In retirement, Caroe gained prominence as a realist commentator on imperial policy, Asian affairs, and western strategy. He contributed regularly to *The Round Table*, the influential journal devoted to Commonwealth affairs, and was the author of three books on the geopolitics of Asia and the Middle East: *Wells of Power* (about Persian

Gulf security), *The Pathans*, and *Soviet Empire: Stalinism and the Turks of Central Asia*.

Caroe was perhaps British India's foremost strategic thinker in the final years before independence. His thought encapsulates the official memory and mindset of the Great Game. In his wartime capacity as foreign secretary, Caroe organized a secret study group to assess the geopolitical implications of postwar independence for India. Caroe's group was based in Delhi and drew its members from the senior ranks of the Indian army as well as from the Indian civil and political services. It met informally and off the record to ensure as candid a discussion as possible. Caroe eventually vetted many of his study group's ideas in his three books and numerous articles. Read collectively, Caroe's public and secret work represents a sort of play-book for the Great Game.

So what according to Caroe were the rules? Caroe is conveniently understood in Mackinderan terms. His wartime study group used the ideas of Sir Halford Mackinder as a springboard for discussion. Historians sometimes portray the Edwardian geographer and pioneer of geopolitical theory as a prophet of containment, but to Caroe, Mackinder embodied the suppositions of more than a century's thought about British India.[4] In fact, Caroe's thinking about the Great Game, like that of his Victorian predecessors, derived substantially from an understanding of Mughal strategy. Central Asia loomed large in the Mughal worldview a young Caroe had read about in the *Akbarnamah*, the famous royal history of the seventeenth century. All Mackinder had done was to make plain what the Mughals implicitly understood: that the "pivot of history" lay in Central Asia. Mackinder saw in Russia's consolidation of Asia's heartland the ultimate challenge to the British Empire. He imagined that from insulated bases in Turkistan, Russia might conquer the Middle East and establish supremacy over China. The effect would be to "overset" the balance of world power.[5] But for the countervailing pressure of Britain's Indian Empire, Russian land power might well have overawed western sea power. At least that is what Olaf Caroe thought.

Caroe recognized that Britain's vaunted command of the sea was interwoven with the defense of South Asia.[6] In his Mackinderan vein of thought, he divided the world into seven "theaters of power." He explained that control of the Indian Ocean theater had, during the nineteenth century, allowed the British to check Russia's gradual absorption of more than half the colossal "central land mass" theater. Control of the Indian Ocean had allowed the British to link the European and Pacific theaters commercially and strategically, giving them a three to one advantage over Russia. Caroe additionally emphasized that control of the Indian Ocean had been a function of an organized subcontinent. Securing the Cape of Good Hope, Suez, and Malacca may have offered sufficient protection against rival navies, but these keys, as the British called them, did not lock all the doors. Caroe argued that land power based in India had offered the only practical way to seal off the most dangerous reentrants. These were situated at the two points where the Indian Ocean theater overlapped the "central land mass" theater: in Afghanistan and in Burma. Such was Caroe's vision as he contemplated the transition from Great Game to Cold War. From his geohistorical standpoint, South Asia appeared not a peripheral zone of international confrontation, but a "central bastion" of world power.[7]

The Soviet invasion of Afghanistan in December 1979 consequently came as small wonder to Caroe. It was exactly the sort of event that he had feared throughout his career would result, not from Britain's withdrawal from South Asia per se, but from a partition of the subcontinent. "If the centre collapses," Caroe wrote about Asia's southern rim in 1969, "the wings are isolated." During the Raj, Afghanistan had survived in equilibrium maintained by setting Indian power against Russian pressure. Twelve years after the liquidation of British rule, "all [was] changed. The counterpoise [had] been removed." Partition had turned the subcontinent in on itself. In Caroe's eyes, August 1947 had seen nothing less than the "negation" of India's power.[8] The only thing he found "surprising" in December 1979 was that it had "taken Russia thirty-two years from the date of independence of the sub-continent to move into Afghanistan." In other words, the Red Army's advance south across the Oxus was but the predictable "after-effect of partition."[9]

Caroe pointed out that from positions in Afghanistan, Russian forces could simultaneously threaten the subcontinent and the vital sea-lanes of the Middle East. He once characterized the Middle East as being "both a vestibule to India and a geographical interspace between the two main systems [of Russian land power and western sea power]."[10] The term "Middle East" was itself an invention of British India. It originally described a problem of the subcontinent's defense, and encompassed a region centered on Iran and Afghanistan.[11] Sistan, a district lying mainly in southwestern Afghanistan but overlapping part of Iran, was the regional pivot.[12] Forces based in Sistan could swing round the great massif of the Hindu Kush to aim at the subcontinent, or point south toward the open ocean outside the Persian Gulf. Lord Curzon, the last Victorian viceroy of India, called Sistan "*terra media* through which any power which is desirous of moving southwards from Meshed, particularly any power that is covetous of an outlet upon the Indian Ocean, must pass."[13]

Caroe similarly predicted that the Russians would try to "advance in a Southern direction much beyond Meshed."[14] Between 1941 and 1945, Meshed, the provincial capital of Khorasan, fell under Russian control as a result of the joint Anglo-Soviet occupation of Iran. As foreign secretary in India, Caroe advised that "whatever else may be predicted of post-war Russia, she will wish to keep open the windows which point her way to the sea."[15] He continued to voice similar concerns in retirement. In fact, Russia's historic drive toward warm water in the south formed a basic theme of *Wells of Power*, Caroe's book on western strategy in the Persian Gulf.

To Caroe, Russian policy in Central Asia seemed part of a larger "*Drang nach Süden*, with the specific object of reaching a port on the Indian Ocean."[16] It is fashionable to suggest that such arguments amount to myth-making, that they reflect a process of "mirror-imaging" British concepts in Russian minds.[17] Caroe's conclusions, however, are hard to dismiss in view of Russian behavior and in light of what evidence there is on the Russian side as to motive. Loath though they were to suggest a move in the face of British strength in India and the Persian Gulf, the tsar's advisors kept an eye on opportunities for expansion. Caroe noted for instance that in 1900 a Russian survey party reconnoitered possible rail routes through eastern Iran from Turkistan to the port of Chah Bahar on the Makran coast.[18] The survey's leader, Captain P. A. Rittich, an intelligence officer attached to the Russian general staff, wrote openly of his country's "ancient dreams of reaching the open ocean in the Middle East."[19] A British military observer who subsequently visited the headquarters of Russia's army on the frontier with eastern Iran reported that the officers he met, junior and senior alike, understood a port on the Indian Ocean to be their "ultimate objective." The British officer added that Chah Bahar was "universally named as the port selected."[20]

In terms of the Cold War, Caroe's argument was that "Russia [would] not dare go to war with the West until she [had] seized the Persian and Arabian oilfields."[21] At least that is how his friend, Lionel Curtis, the doyen of imperial reform, summarized *Wells of Powers*. Caroe's view may in hindsight appear vintage Cold War realism. Certainly the vision was not particularly innovative. Caroe himself described the Middle Eastern imperatives of the Cold War as "new wine in old bottles."[22] Yet *Wells of Power* was a criticism of Anglo-American strategy, not a summary. Caroe assumed that, as Curtis put it, "the real strategic facts with which the [west] has to deal are not with Berlin but with the Middle East."[23] The trouble was Caroe's surmise was not exactly the supposition that informed the mainline of Anglo-American war planning in the early phase of the Cold War.

The British had played the Great Game on the premise that Russia's road to London ran through Tehran, Kabul, and Delhi. Caroe expected the Soviets similarly to make a bid for predominance in Europe by applying pressure in the East. Allied war planners, however, anticipated a more direct approach from the enemy in the event of actual hostilities. In the years between 1945 and 1954, during which Caroe published *Wells of Power*, the preferred scenario for a Third World War envisaged the Soviets lunging immediately into Western Europe and advancing in the Middle East as a rear-guard action.

Anglo-American war planners looked on the Middle East not so much as a great reservoir of oil as the critical region from which a strategic air campaign would be mounted to reverse Soviet aggression. From bases in Egypt and the Levant, Allied air power could launch missions to cripple Russia's oil production by knocking out the all-important cluster of refineries in Ukraine.[24] South Asia figured in the scheme, at least initially, as the necessary base area from which to attack secondary targets behind the Urals.[25] In a sense, Allied air strategy represented in itself a rediscovery of the Great Game. As one Indian observer has put it, the rise of air power "led to a revival of the Palmerstonian Forward Policy with a vigour that no one could have predicted."[26] Lord Palmerston, the great Victorian statesman, had been a leading proponent of developing a sufficient military presence along Russia's southern flank that Britain could if necessary carry a war straight into the Eurasian heartland.[27]

Despite all this, Caroe showed considerable perspicacity in the pattern he and his Victorian predecessors in British India had anticipated. A strategic survey of Iran completed by the Soviet general staff in early 1941 explicitly detailed how Meshed's capture would establish a base for operations against Sistan and ultimately Chah Bahar.[28] During their occupation of Afghanistan in the 1980s, the Soviets constructed large air bases just north of Sistan at Farah and Shindand. From these facilities, high-performance jets could reach the Hormuz oil bottleneck in under an hour, and Soviet naval bombers and patrol planes were in range of the Indian Ocean.[29] Setting aside the obvious technological differences, the deployment and disposition of Soviet strategic projection forces in Afghanistan were right along the lines that Field Marshal Lord Roberts, Commander-in-Chief of the Indian army, had forecast a hundred years earlier in 1885. Roberts predicted that in the event of an invasion, "Russian outposts would be pushed forward to Farah."[30]

Caroe saw the Great Game as an "early variation of a cold war with Russia." He perceived constancy in Russia and the danger of a consolidated Asian heartland. "We must not think," he told a London audience in 1949, "that that continental view has not got a permanent validity and importance, because it has, and all the more so now that the shadows are lengthening from the north."[31] Caroe was a stalwart anticommunist, but he always held that Soviet expansion was rooted at least as much in the Russian past as in Marxist ideology. "Tsarist or Soviet, 1600 or 1950," he posited, "Russian technique and Russian reactions are much the same. Russian policy is indeed perpetual."[32]

In the wake of the Soviet Union's disintegration, it is tempting, even fashionable, to dismiss such views as antiquated. To say that Caroe recognized constancy in Russian policy is not, however, to mean that he believed in the implacability of Russian power. In fact, the events of the early 1990s would probably have no more surprised him than did those of the late 1970s. When in the 1950s many saw only the inexorability of international communism, Caroe recognized Russia's ultimate difficulty in forcibly holding a multiethnic empire in Central Asia together. He maintained that "even if Russian domination were assured, the people of Turkistan will not forget their freedom so far as to renounce their languages and their faith." Caroe predicted that eventually the "tide [would] turn" against Moscow.[33] It is telling that he chose as his analogy the perpetual ebb and flow of the ocean. Communism would one day recede; yes, but might not Russia surge back in? Caroe had witnessed the cycle within the span of his own Indian career. As a soldier during the First World War, he had seen Russia lose her grip on Central Asia altogether. For a brief period during 1918 and 1919, he had even seen British and Indian forces occupy the Caucasus oil center of Baku and portions of Transcaspia. A decade later, as a political officer on India's Afghan border, Caroe found himself dealing with the acutely felt danger posed by a reconsolidated and reinvigorated Russian empire in Central Asia.

One can only speculate where Caroe would weigh in on today's debate about a possible revivification of Russian imperialism, but it seems safe to say that talk of a "New Great Game" for control of Caspian oil and gas is perfectly consistent with Caroe's view of the Asian scene.[34] It is interesting to note that the very routes which long ago channeled Mongol armies into India and later threatened to funnel the tsar's cavalry and Soviet armor southward from Central Asia remain the subject of intense speculation, albeit as energy carriers. Where the last century proved an age of empire, the next promises an era of emerging markets. Pipeline builders and portfolio managers have replaced the military topographers and diplomatists of the Raj, but the landscape and politics so familiar to Olaf Caroe and earlier Imperial officers endure. The Great Game pattern did not unravel with the Cold War's end. It will endure in any coming Pacific Century.

The Cold War has so conditioned the historiography of the Great Game that one tends to miss how wide the British/Indian vision was. Lieutenant-General Sir Francis Tuker, a member of Caroe's wartime study group, conveyed the scope. "The defence of the 'the East'," he wrote, "is one complete strategical problem."[35] It will be recalled that Caroe pictured "India at the centre of an Asiatic system."[36] Afghanistan was but one of two landward reentrants that he identified in the Indian Ocean theater. The other was Burma, where the great Irrawaddy cut a second corridor from Central Asia to the sea. Russia reaching warm water on South Asia's western flank was not the only danger that worried Caroe. From early in his career, he consistently advised that however more immediate it seemed, the threat in the Middle East must not distract from the watch on the subcontinent's eastern gates. The Japanese army underscored the point in 1942, when it swept across Southeast Asia to India's doorstep. In Caroe's view, there could be no choosing between "leaving the Himalayas open to China and the Indian Ocean to Russian fleets."[37]

Although holding the Asian rim represented a single problem, Caroe considered China independently of Russia and international communism. He did envision "some move toward a concordat between China and Russia along the lines of the abortive Molotov-Ribbentrop pact." And he supposed that "such an agreement might leave Nepal and all to the east of it to China, Kashmir and the lands towards the Gulf to Soviet penetration." But he did not see a monolithic threat. Chinese interests ultimately drove Chinese policy, whatever ideological affinity Peking shared with Moscow. Caroe recognized that Mao Zedong's "Chinese dynasty, like others before it, will aspire to the leadership of Asia, and is likely to regard India as effete, Russia as an interloper, and many of the small Asian states such as Nepal and Burma as potential satellites."[38] During the Second World War, years before the communist takeover, he repeatedly stressed his sense that "history had proved that there was such a thing as Chinese imperialism."[39] Ten years later, Caroe emphasized that "like Tsarist Russia,

Imperial China was always expansionist in Inner Asia as opportunity offered and strength allowed. That tradition holds in Communist China."[40]

During the Second World War, even as the Japanese army bore down on India, there was considerable speculation among Caroe's circle in Delhi about the latent, long-term danger of "greater China." The diaspora of overseas Chinese in Southeast Asia seemed an "ideal fifth column." Referring to them as the "Sudetan [*sic*] Chinese," one member of Caroe's study group conjured the image of Nazi machinations, while Caroe himself warned of a "Chinese Ausland organisation."[41] What had given rise to such allusions was Chiang Kai-shek's publication in 1943 of *China's Destiny*.[42] The Generalissimo's book seemed all too "reminiscent of German *Geopolitik*."[43] Caroe told authorities in London that the book left "little doubt that Chinese imperialist and irredentist sentiment has hardened."[44] Even before Chiang's book, however, members of Caroe's study group already suspected that revanchism imbued the nationalism of a waking China. They worried especially about what appeared a "nascent Chinese imperialism which is not disinclined to regard Burma as its natural frontier and demands not only the reopening of the Burma Road but the permanent retention of the port of Rangoon."[45]

The key to Burma was China's province of Yunnan. Like Sistan in the Middle East, Yunnan formed a regional pivot. Caroe and his study group feared that from a reconsolidated and insulated position in Yunnan, China might aim toward the Indian Ocean by way of the Irrawaddy valley or, by debouching on eastern Tibet, look down the Brahmaputra valley into the very of heart of India itself. At the same time, bases in Yunnan might point China's path to the waters around Indochina by the route of either the Mekong or Hong river.

In fact, Caroe's study group attributed considerable importance to Vietnam as a necessary outwork of India's defense. Caroe's military colleague, Lieutenant-General Sir Francis Tuker, wrote that air power based in Vietnam could "throttle the naval power of maneuver of a reborn China."[46] Another member of Caroe's study group speculated that a hitherto undeveloped harbor on the Vietnamese coast had "all the natural qualities to be the naval base for dominating the South China Seas."[47] Its name was Cam Ranh, and it would eventually become the site of a major American complex subsequently exploited by the strategic projection forces of the Soviet Union.

Today, China is insinuating its economic influence throughout northern Burma. Mandalay, in the heart of the country, has become a focus of Chinese investment. Chinese engineers are surveying the Irrawaddy, possibly with a mind to opening a riverine link between Yunnan and the Indian Ocean. Rumors abound of China's ultimate military designs on Burma. China has constructed what defense analysts in both India and the West describe as a "maritime reconnaissance facility" on Burma's Great Coco Island in the Bay of Bengal. Meanwhile, reports that the Chinese navy is interested in bases along Burma's coast and in access to the Mergui Archipelago, near the northern approach to the busy Strait of Malacca, have become routine. Just what China's object is remains unclear, but surveillance of India's military complex at Port Blair, tracking Indian missile tests in Orissa, and keeping a not necessarily benign eye on shipping are all suspected purposes.[48]

In any case, China's interest in Burma and courtship of its pariah regime have added considerable fuel to ongoing predictions in American policy circles of a "coming conflict with China."[49] In India, China's approach in Burma has reinforced misgivings dating to the 1962 war between the two Asian giants. The accession of India's Bharatia Janata Party government in early 1998 brought worries about Chinese ambitions back to the fore of Indian policy. In explaining India's decision in May 1998 to test nuclear weapons, Prime Minister Atal Vajpayee and other spokesmen have stressed concern about the growth of Chinese power as an essential motive. When he stated in the spring of 1998 that "China is potential threat number one," India's defense minister talked as much about Chinese involvement in Burma as in Pakistan.[50]

The current debate over the direction a waking China will take has a clear antecedent in the wartime deliberations of officials in British India. One line of opinion in Caroe's study group advocated "engagement," to use a 1990s' phrase. They imagined a "Sino-British entente" and the inclusion of China in a multilateral framework for Indian Ocean security. They even suggested the possibility of conceding to China "dominant influence" in Burma. This advice appalled authorities in London. One reckoned that the entente faction's imagined "end of imperialism" in Southeast Asia would in practice amount only to "its replacement by a nice incompetent Chinese imperialism."[51] For his own part, Caroe was equally skeptical. "We need the co-operation of China," he admitted, "but we shall not obtain it, much less the loyal support of the border States, by a negative policy of submitting to encroachment."[52] He explained that "lacking a firm bastion in Burma, the eastern approaches to India could never be secure." Burma, Caroe insisted, formed a "most necessary barrier between India and the ambition of China."[53]

The wartime debate over China had antecedents of its own in Victorian and Edwardian thinking. Some strategists of the Raj, like the inimitable trans-Himalayan explorer Sir Francis Younghusband, advised playing what in Cold War parlance would be called the "China card." Younghusband urged that Britain promote China's power in Central Asia as a counterweight to Russia.[54] Others, like British military intelligence chief Major-General Sir John Ardagh, warned about the "futility of trusting to [China] as a possible ally." Ardagh feared that China would prove "useless as a buffer between Russia and Northern India."[55] A few went even further, forecasting the possibility of an active Chinese threat to India. Colonel Sir Thomas Holdich, perhaps the era's leading expert on the military geography of South Asia, considered such a development highly improbable. Nonetheless, he felt "bound to admit that it might be possible for an unopposed Chinese force to invade India by Eastern Tibet; possibly even by the valley of Assam."[56]

Among those Victorians to sense an emerging Chinese danger was Sir Alfred Lyall. Caroe regarded Lyall, who served as British India's foreign secretary between 1878 and 1881, as both a personal role model and the most far-seeing of all his predecessors. Writing in 1905, Lyall warned that "as on [India's] north-western frontier we are very sensitive to the vicinity of Russia, so on [India's] border-line in the north-east of Burmah [*sic*] we begin to feel distinctly, the presence of that great organized State, the most ancient upon earth, which has so long dominated on that side of Asia—the Chinese empire."[57] Lyall added rather ominously that "the Chinese emperor had been accustomed to claim certain formal acknowledgments of traditional allegiance" from the Burmese state.[58]

A century earlier, while the soldiers of the East India Company remained busy fencing with Indian princes and parrying French rivals, Qing armies were at war in central Burma. The point is that South Asia was a focus of world power long before the Cold War, and even before the Raj. Mughal or Victorian, Russian or Chinese, geopolitics transcends period. It is the continuity of strategic imperatives that Olaf Caroe's vision of the Great Game helps to elucidate as we contemplate a Pacific Century. Though its form may change, as in the Cold War, something of the Great Game is likely to persist. In this message, Caroe echoes Rudyard Kipling's admonition in *Kim*: "When everyone is dead the Great Game is finished. Not before."[59]

# REFERENCES

1. [Olaf Caroe], "Buffer States: Their Historic Service to Peace," *The Round Table*, n. 180 (1955): 344.

2. Robert J. McMahon, *The Cold War on the Periphery: The United States, India, and Pakistan* (New York: Columbia Univ. Press, 1994), 344.

3. Caroe to Peel, 19 December 1944, IO L/P&S/12/727. Abbreviations: CAB = Cabinet Office files, PRO = Public Record Office, Kew; IO = India Office files, British Museum, London; MSS Eur. = European Manuscript collections, British Museum, London; WO = War Office files, Public Record Office, Kew.

4. The Mackinderan framework, which never really fell off scope of geographers and political scientists, is currently enjoying something of a rediscovery among historians. See especially John LeDonne, *The Russian Empire and the World, 1700–1917: The Geopolitics of Expansion and Containment* (Oxford: Oxford Univ. Press, 1997); Milan Hauner, *What Is Asia to Us?: Russia's Asian Heartland Yesterday and Today* (London: Routledge, 1990); and Christopher Bellamy, "Struggle for the Asian Heartland," *The Spectator*, 15 March 1997. For Mackinder as prophet, Paul Kennedy, *The Rise and Fall of British Naval Mastery* (London: Allen Lane, 1976).

5. The essential introductions to Mackinder's thought are Halford J. Mackinder, *Democratic Ideals and Reality* (London: Constable, 1919); H. J. Mackinder, "The Geographical Pivot of History," *The Geographical Journal*, 23, 4 (1904); and H. J. Mackinder, "The Round World and the Winning of the Peace," *Foreign Affairs*, 21, 4 (1943). The best secondary overviews are Brian W. Blouet, *Halford Mackinder: A Biography* (College Station: Texas A & M Press, 1987); James T. Lowe, *Geopolitics and War: Mackinder's Philosophy of Power* (Washington, DC: Univ. Press of America, 1981); and W. H. Parker, *Mackinder as an Aid to Statecraft* (Oxford: Oxford Univ. Press, 1982). For Mackinder's place in the wider spectrum on geopolitical thought, Geoffrey Parker, *Western Geopolitical Thought in the Twentieth Century* (New York: St. Martin's Press, 1985).

6. For a provocative discussion of the relative importance of India and naval supremacy to Britain's world power, Edward Ingram, *Commitment to Empire: Prophecies of the Great Game in Asia, 1797–1800* (Oxford: Oxford Univ. Press, 1981). Ingram's book is usefully balanced by Piers Mackesy, *War Without Victory: The Downfall of Pitt, 1799–1802* (Oxford: Oxford Univ. Press, 1984).

7. Olaf Caroe, "Problems of Power Confrontation in Inner Asia," *Journal of the Royal Central Asian Society*, 56, 3 (1969): 221. For Caroe's elaboration of the "theaters of power," "The North-West Frontier," lecture by Olaf Caroe, 6 April 1949, MSS Eur. F.203/47 (Caroe Papers, British Museum); Olaf Caroe, *Wells of Power: The Oilfields of South-Western Asia: A Regional and Global Study* (London: Macmillan, 1951); and [Olaf Caroe], "Arabia Felix and the Indian Ocean: A Study of Political Strategy," *The Round Table*, 216 (1964). Caroe adopted the phrase "theaters of power" from H. V. Hodson, who was among the original members of Caroe's wartime study group in India. See H. V. Hodson, *Twentieth Century Empire* (London: Faber & Faber, 1948). Similar ideas were put forward in a book by Lieutenant-General Sir Francis Tuker, another member of Caroe's study group. See Francis Tuker, *Does Stalin Mean War?* (London: Batchworth Press, 1952). The early development of

the "theaters of power" concept can be followed in the memoranda of Caroe's study group: "Whither India's Foreign Policy?" memorandum by Caroe, 26 April 1942, IO L/P&S/12/724; "A Post-War System of Security for the Indian Ocean," memorandum by Hodson, undated [1942], IO L/P&S/12/724; "Some Political and Constitutional Reflections on the Landward Security of the India of the Future," memorandum by Caroe, 18 August 1944, IO L/P&S/12/727; and "The Future of War and the Future of an Army," memorandum by Tuker, December 1944, IO L/P&S/12/730B.

8. Caroe, "Problems of Power Confrontation in Inner Asia": 221.

9. Olaf Caroe, "The Strategic After-Effects of India's Partition," *The Round Table*, 180, (1955): 344.

10. [Olaf Caroe], "Buffer States . . . ": 344.

11. General Sir Thomas Edward Gordon, an officer of the Indian army, was the first to use the term "Middle East" in print. He did so in 1900. Alfred Thayer Mahan, the American naval theorist, and Sir Valentine Chirol, the famous Edwardian correspondent of *The Times*, subsequently popularized the phrase. See T. E. Gordon, "The Problem of the Middle East," *The Nineteenth Century*, March 1900; A. T. Mahan, The Problem of Asia and Its Effect Upon International Policies (Boston: Little, Brown, 1900); A. T. Mahan, "The Persian Gulf and International Relations," *The National Review*, September 1902; and Valentine Chirol, *The Middle Eastern Question and Some Problems of Indian Defence* (London: John Murray, 1903). For an overview of the issue, Clayton R. Koppes, "Captain Mahan, General Gordon, and the Origins of the Term 'Middle East'," *Middle Eastern Studies*, 12, 1 (1976).

12. For an overview of the problem, Rose L. Greaves, "Sistan in British Indian Frontier Policy," *Bulletin of the School of Oriental and African Studies*, 49, 1 (1986).

13. George N. Curzon, *Persia and the Persian Question* (London: Longmans, Green, 1892), 235.

14. External Affairs Department [Caroe] to Secretary of State, 10 September 1941, IO L/P&S/12/3519.

15. "The essential interests of the British Commonwealth in the Persian Gulf and its coastal states, with special reference to India," memorandum by Caroe, 1944, IO L/P&S/12/3519.

16. Caroe, *Wells of Power*, 197–198.

17. For example, William Green, "The Historic Russian Drive for a Warm Water Port: Anatomy of a Geopolitical Myth," *Naval War College Review*, 46, 2 (1993).

18. Caroe, *Wells of Power*, 64–67.

19. Quoted in Milan Hauner, *What Is Asia to Us?*, 104.

20. "Russian Interests in the Middle East," memorandum by Whyte, 6 June 1903, CAB 6/1.

21. Curtis to Holliday, 23 March 1949, MSS Eur. F.203/47 [Caroe Papers, British Museum].

22. [Olaf Caroe], "The Persian Gulf: A Romance," *The Round Table*, 154 (1949): 136.

23. Curtis to Head, 31 January 1949, MSS Eur. F.203/47 [Caroe Papers, British Museum].

24. See Michael J. Cohen, *Fighting World War Three from the Middle East: Allied Contingency Plans, 1945–1954* (London: Frank Cass, 1997).

25. See R. J. Aldrich, and M. Coleman, "Britain and the Strategic Air Of-

fensive Against the Soviet Union: The Question of South Asian Air Bases, 1945–1949," *History*, 74 (1989).

26. Prem Shankar Jha, *Kashmir 1947: Rival Versions of History* (Delhi: Oxford Univ. Press, 1996), p. 85.

27. On such thinking, G. J. Alder, "India and the Crimean War," *Journal of Imperial and Commonwealth History*, 2 (1973).

28. Gerald Guensburg (trans.), *Soviet Command Study of Iran, 1941* (Arlington: SRI International, 1980).

29. See Yossef Bodansky, "Soviet Military Operations in Afghanistan," in Rosanne Klass (ed.), *Afghanistan: The Great Game Revisited* (New York: Freedom House, 1987); Milan Hauner, "Seizing the Third Parallel: Geopolitics and the Soviet Advance into Central Asia," *Orbis*, Spring 1985; and Eric Margolis, "The Next Soviet Lake?" *U.S. Naval Institute Proceedings*, March 1987.

30. "What are Russia's vulnerable points? And how have they affected our Afghan frontier policy?" memorandum by Roberts, 1885, WO 110/9/4296.

31. "The North-West Frontier," lecture by Caroe, 6 April 1949, MSS Eur. F.203/47 [Caroe Papers, British Museum].

32. Caroe, *Wells of Power*, 77.

33. Olaf Caroe, *Soviet Empire: The Turks of Central Asia and Stalinism* (London: Macmillan, 1953), 268.

34. For an overview, Geoffrey Kemp and Robert E. Harkavy, *Strategic Geography and the Changing Middle East* (Washington: Carnegie Endowment, 1997). Also, Ahmed Rashid, "The New Great Game," *Far Eastern Economic Review*, 10 April 1997.

35. Note by Tuker, enclosed in Caroe to Peel, 28 February 1945, IO L/P&S/12/727.

36. Caroe to Donaldson, 13 September 1945, IO L/P&S/12/3547.

37. Caroe, "Problems of Power Confrontation in Inner Asia," 225.

38. Caroe, 225.

39. Quoted in Christopher Thorne, *Allies of a Kind: The United States, Britain, and the War Against Japan* (Oxford: Oxford Univ. Press, 1978), 310.

40. Letter by Caroe, *The Times*, 4 November 1954.

41. "Modern China's Asiatic Empire," anonymous memorandum [by Wint], 20 March 1945, IO L/P&S/12/730B; Caroe to Cleary, 19 June 1945, IO L/P&S/12/729.

42. Two English translations were published in 1947. The version authorized by the KMT is Wang Chung-hui (trans.), Chiang Kai-shek, *China's Destiny* (New York: Macmillan, 1947). The second and unauthorized version is Philip Jaffe (trans.), Chiang Kai-shek, *China's Destiny* (New York: Roy Publishers, 1947).

43. "Modern China's Asiatic Empire," anonymous memorandum [by Wint], 20 March 1945, IO L/P&S/12/730B.

44. Caroe to Peel, 19 September 1945, IO L/P&S/12/4195A.

45. "India's Relation to the Far East," memorandum by Gregory, 19 August 1942, IO L/P&S/12/725.

46. "The Future of War and the Future of an Army," memorandum by Tuker, December 1944, IO L/P&S/12/730B.

47. "Burma, Siam, Indo-China, Malaya," memorandum by Wint, undated [1945], IO L/P&S/12/730B.

48. For a judicious overview, Donald M. Seekins, "Burma-China Relations: Playing with Fire," *Asian Survey*, v. 37, n. 6, 1997. For the Indian dimension, Andrew Selth, "Burma and the Strategic Competition between China and India," *Journal of Strategic Studies*, 19, 2 (1996).

49. See especially Richard Bernstein and Ross H. Munro, *The Coming Conflict with China* (New York: Knopf, 1997). For China as a conservative versus revisionist power, Andrew J. Nathan and Robert S. Ross, *The Great Wall and the Empty Fortress: China's Search for Security* (New York: Norton, 1997). For an introduction to the historical context of thinking on Chinese expansion in Britain and British India, Charles A. Fisher, "Containing China I: The Antecedents of Containment," *Geographical Journal*, 136 (1970); and Charles A. Fisher, "Containing China II: Concepts and Applications of Containment," *Geographical Journal*, 137 (1971).

50. "George in the China Shop," *India Today*, 18 May 1998.

51. Minutes of discussion, Viceroy's Study Group, 20 August 1942, IO L/P&S/12/725; and marginal notations by Rumbold on "A Post-War Security System for the Indian Ocean," memorandum by Hodson, 1942, IO L/P&S/12/724.

52. "India and the Mongolian Fringe," memorandum by Caroe, 18 January 1940, IO L/P&S/12/725.

53. Minutes of discussion, Viceroy's Study Group, 23 September 1942, IO L/P&S/12/725.

54. For Younghusband's views, Parshotam Mehra, *An "Agreed" Frontier: Ladakh and India's Northern Most Borders, 1846–1947* (Delhi: Oxford University Press, 1992), ch. 7.

55. "The Northern Frontier of India from the Pamirs to Tibet", memorandum by Ardagh, 1 January 1897, in Mehra, *An "Agreed" Frontier*, appendix 10.

56. Thomas Holdich, *The Gates of India* (London: Macmillan, 1910), 188.

57. Alfred Lyall, *The Rise and Expansion of British Dominion in India* (London: John Murray, 1907), 339.

58. Alfred Lyall, *The Life of the Marquis of Dufferin and Ava*, v. 2 (London: John Murray, 1905), 132.

59. Rudyard Kipling, *Kim* (New York: Oxford Univ. Press, 1995, originally 1901), 234.

# 7
# JOYCE CARY'S *MISTER JOHNSON* AND THE TOOLS OF EMPIRE

**Barry J. Ward**

> Among the many important events of the nineteenth century, two were of momentous consequence for the entire world. One was the progress and power of industrial technology; the other was the domination and exploitation of Africa and Asia by Europeans.
>
> Daniel R. Headrick
> *The Tools of Empire*

Joyce Cary's *Mister Johnson* can be read for what it reveals about the ways the British Empire actually functioned in early twentieth-century West Africa. The novel records the story of the building of the Fada Road in Borgu, a remote area in northwestern Nigeria previously isolated from the changes in trade, transport, and government experienced by the rest of the country. The road, the brainchild of District Officer Rudbeck and his clerk, Johnson, is opposed by the local emir who rightly perceives it to be a threat to his power. More than the emir can know, infrastructure development such as roads will open the door for western industrial technology to change Africa as the road leads to trade and contact with the outside world. Cary's depiction of the Fada Road as opening up Borgu to the wider world of Nigeria and the British Empire is a brilliant study of how the "tools of empire" played a major role in its expansion. A knowledge of empire policies on road building helps illuminate the novel, and the novel in turn gives dramatic realization to these policies.

## THE QUESTION OF CLERK JOHNSON

At first sight the plot of *Mister Johnson* seems to consist of a series of sharply defined rises and falls in Clerk Johnson's fortunes. Johnson serves as Rudbeck's right-hand man and the escort of the District Officer's newly arrived wife, Celia. During one of Rudbeck's absences Johnson is dismissed by Assistant District Officer Tring for embezzlement, then taken in by the storeowner Gollup who first trusts and later fires him. Upon Rudbeck's return Johnson helps him create the road and is once again dismissed for using *zungo*, travelers's lodges, money to pay for the road gang's beer. Later still, he successfully robs Gollup's store before eventually being caught in the act by Gollup, whom he murders in self-defense. Johnson is arrested, tried, and finally executed. This pattern of ups and downs represents Johnson's fate from the point of view of Ajali, the conservative store clerk with a vindictive sense of justice, who anxiously awaits Johnson's downfall. When the narrative point of view returns to Johnson, the inadequacy of this interpretation is made apparent. The force of Johnson's character is such that what from Ajali's point of view has been a tale of petty misdemeanor escalating into murder, becomes, in Johnson's telling, an entertaining adventure.[1] Tragically, that adventure culminates in misunderstanding and the hero's death. We recognize that Johnson is a casualty of empire, one of the countless individuals who run afoul of the "civilizing" process imposed by an alien western power. The enduring appeal of Johnson's charm is, of course, that he is not just a victim but an unforgettable character, a life force next to whom other characters in the novel pale. He possesses what Cary believes is the artist's extraordinary resilience, a strength enhanced by the fact of Johnson's capacity to live in the present moment. As Cary says, "to him Africa is simply perpetual experience, exciting, amusing, alarming or delightful, which he soaks into himself throughout all his five senses at once, and produces again in the form of reflections, comments, songs, jokes, all in the pure Johnsonian form."[2]

Johnson's personal problems are also Africa's. He is Africa with all its vitality, exasperation, disappointments, and tragedies. His, and Africa's, incredible history is one of idealism, energy, and vision blasted by folly, avarice, and misunderstanding. Johnson's machinations are the product of individual artistic creativity, and historical and economic factors already in place when Cary became a district officer in Nigeria in 1914.

Cary's *Mister Johnson* has generated heated debate over its characterization of Clerk Johnson and its portrayal of West Africa. Declaring the ultimate futility of settling the argument over Johnson's character and authenticity, Robert Wren proposes that the novel is not about Johnson at all, that he can be safely disregarded as a purely instrumental agent for Rudbeck, "colonial officer, symbol and activist of Progress."[3] The book, Wren continues, is about Rudbeck and about the **road** that Rudbeck wants to build. Rudbeck will build the road, he tells us, "not because a road is needed, not because it is ordered, but because—in some unarticulated way—he thinks that to build a Road is Good."[4]

Notwithstanding Wren's neocolonialist impulse to supplant an African protagonist with a European one, his emphasis on the importance of the road is well placed. The planning and execution of road construction are important structural elements in the novel, and the road's symbolic significance is central to the meaning of the story. It is preposterous, of course, to state that Johnson can be disregarded, that he is merely Rudbeck's instrument. The drive to build the road is as much Johnson's as Rudbeck's. Johnson, more than Rudbeck, serves as the agent of progress, and it is the road, not Rudbeck, that is progress's symbol and tool. The road, in its construction and upon its completion, functions as an instrument of power and an emblem of empire.

Literary scholars have recognized the Fada Road as broadly symbolic. William van O'Connor concludes that "the road itself is symbolic, an act of creation. It opens up the bush for trade, for social intercourse, for new experiences, for [western] civilization. It also brings social evils."[5] This is, of course, self-evident; even Rudbeck understands as much. When Wren locates the road's significance not in its creative powers but in the attendant social evils of opening Borgu with a road, he asks us to believe that *Mister Johnson* is an unintended bitter critique of British colonialism and its agents. This is a remarkable charge to lay upon Joyce Cary, that he was in fact a closet anti-imperialist who wrote a subversive novel about the British colonial enterprise in Africa. However he may have tempered his enthusiasm for Lord Lugard's policy of indirect rule or the possibilities for achieving liberal social aims in Africa by the 1930s, Cary never consciously repudiated his belief in furthering the empire or the underlying assumptions of late nineteenth- and early twentieth-century colonial policy.

Still, one senses the ambivalence in Cary's presentation of Johnson and the empire, an ambivalence which can be accounted for in at least two ways. First, Cary is writing the novel in 1937, nearly two decades after his years in Nigeria and in a period when the empire itself is shutting down. Policy failures in Africa are evident, and the views the young District Officer Cary once held have been severely tested. Second, Cary never was entirely able to get over his feeling that he was a kind of casualty of empire himself, one who was dispossessed of his Irish legacy by rent laws enacted by the British Parliament. Barbara

Fisher describes the tension Cary felt living "between two irreconcilable worlds," Ireland and England, and the distress he expressed over the fate of his grandfather ruined by rent laws legislation. Indeed, Cary spent the years up to his mid-forties calling himself an Irishman.[6] Only later in life did he take up an English identity.[7] He actually seems to have spent most of his life feeling dislodged from his rightful place in society. Furthermore, as an artist in a relentlessly commercial age, he had to collaborate with the business classes who published and sold his work. His early potboilers were sold to *The Saturday Evening Post*, an American magazine that paid well over British market prices. But he eventually learned that the reading public could not be counted on to support a writer of short stories. Cary's full measure of public acclaim and wealth came only when he began giving the public what it (and the publishers) wanted —full length novels, the requisite means for establishing himself as a "brand name" which could command respect—and reward—in the literary marketplace. Thus, however much of a conscious imperialist Cary might have been as a young man on the spot in Borgu or as a fifty-year old apologist for liberal ideology,[8] he has to have been rather more conflicted on a subconscious level. After all, he was a dispossessed member of the Protestant Ascendancy and a struggling artist whose commitment to his craft was at odds with the practical demands of a commercial society which expected him to be able to pay his rates and the school fees for his four sons.[9]

In the context of Cary's criticism, conscious or not, of the British Empire, several relevant questions arise about the road as a symbol of progress and tool of empire. Why did Rudbeck build the road? Why did Johnson collaborate in the enterprise? What does the technology of road (and bridge) building mean in terms of colonial development in Nigeria? And, how do such literary representations of the relationship of technology to empire lead to a rediscovery of the continued importance of the British Empire? First some studies of the impact of western technology on European colonies in Africa.

## TECHNOLOGY AND EMPIRE

*Tools of Empire* author Daniel Headrick builds a persuasive case for the central role of technology in the development of European imperialism. "What the breechloader, the machine gun, the steamboat and steamship, and quinine and other innovations did," he explains, "was to lower the cost, in both financial and human terms [for the colonizers], of penetrating, conquering, and exploiting new territories."[10] The application of western technology in Africa and Asia made imperial conquest so cheap in terms of western lives lost that domestic political dissent melted away and nations were moved to add new territories to those already under their colonial control.[11] *The Tentacles of Progress*, Headrick's second book on technology, further explores the forms and extent of technological penetration by considering the roles of ships, telecommunications systems, agricultural innovations, railroads and, by extension, roads and motor vehicles. If one looks at how European technological penetration played out in Africa, development became nearly synonymous with the employment of technologies in the service of military aims, the increase of trade and its consequent tax revenues, and the support of cultural regeneration which Europeans thought necessary for their subject peoples. Technology, Headrick concludes, has transformed the modern world more than leaders, religious beliefs, or armed conflicts. The effects of technological innovation on eighteenth-century England provide a preview of the changes Rudbeck and Johnson's road are likely to have on Nigeria, especially on class structure and urbanization. R. A. Buchanan describes the change in England as no less than a revolution. "Modern social classes" he tells us,

> are the creation of the processes of rapid industrialization . . . Eighteenth century society was still dominated by a hereditary, landowning, aristocracy. Social distinctions were thus distinctions of caste rather than class, being too rigid to permit mobility between different social levels except in very limited respects. This society was disrupted by the emergence of the new social classes . . . so that, in the most general sense, technology can be said to have precipitated a political revolution.[12]

If Headrick and Buchanan are even partially correct in their assessment of the transformational power of western technology, one might assume that technology and its effects would find a place in literature inspired by the colonial experience. In the case of Joyce Cary, this is especially true as he was both a political agent of British colonialism and a novelist whose subject was the colonial scene. In order to facilitate the movement of men and merchandise, to industrialize Africa, and to stimulate trade, roads are essential. Lacking adequate transport, people cannot travel to seek work or conduct trade beyond local markets.[13]

## A CHANGE IN THE OFFICIAL MIND

The British Empire had but limited colonial interests in West Africa when it ended British participation in the slave trade with the Act of 1807. Disengagement from the business of slave sale and transport was neither easy nor immediate. European and American ships continued to ply the coast, much to the dismay and indignation of abolitionists in England. Colonial bases, established to combat the slave trade, became centers for the promotion of legal trade and development.[14] Thus, the termination of the slave trade began a process of West African colonial expansion, which, one hundred years later, had engulfed the entire continent. Early in the nineteenth century a variety of far-reaching, laissez-faire economic reforms were introduced. The protective tariffs favored by mercantilists were eliminated, as were a number of trading preferences. Bans on the transfer of advanced technology were lifted.[15] In the 1820s the Navigation Acts were repealed as a step toward free trade.[16] It seemed self-evident to the British at the time that, as Paul Kennedy ironically described it, ". . . over time everybody would surely recognize the fundamental validity of laissez-faire economics and utilitarian codes of government."[17]

Even so, policies of informal empire such as free trade and open markets did not lead to the economic development or social liberation promised by their advocates. In mid-century, British trade with most of West Africa was insignificant, and internal African strife led to a reconsideration of early colonial ventures. By 1865 a select committee of the House of Commons recommended ultimate withdrawal from all West African colonies. Because humanitarian and some commercial interests (especially those profiting from the palm oil trade) resisted such plans for abandonment and since the British saw the value of these colonies for the defense of their sea lanes to India, the committee recommendation was not acted upon, and free trade policies remained in effect in spite of economic stagnation.[18] As Robinson and Gallagher indicate in *Africa and the Victorians*, "On the eve of the Scramble Lagos was still regarded as an [economic] liability."[19]

A critical change in colonial policy toward Africa occurred in 1895. Previously neither Whitehall nor the Colonial Office had seen any need for government intervention to develop the economic potential of the African colonies. These colonies had been acquired primarily for humanitarian and geopolitical reasons, not economic ones, and if economic development were to take place, British policy makers saw it as the role and responsibility of private enterprise. "The merchant," it was assumed, "was expected to create empire . . . to pioneer his own way inland."[20]

Appointment of Joseph Chamberlain to the Colonial Office in 1895 marked a change in this longstanding policy. Free trade policies, effective for England so long as she held sway as the world's foremost economic power, were reversed in the face of new competition from developing industrial rivals such as Germany, the United States, and Japan. As Chamberlain indicated in a communique to the West African Railways Deputation, the progress and prosperity of Great Britain depended on the expansion and economic development of the empire [24 Aug. 1895].[21] Tropical Africa could no longer remain outside the market for British industry and, Chamberlain argued, as had already happened in India as of 1858, "the state must take the lead in empire-building from the merchant and investor."[22]

Since private enterprise had not been able to expand West African markets, Chamberlain declared that the British government must fund the development of infrastructure. Resistance to direct government investment came from Prime Minister Salisbury and other conservative colonialists of an earlier era who doubted that investment in Africa would pay sufficient dividends. Nonetheless, the new economic realities for which Chamberlain stood prevailed and the British government got into the business of building roads, railroads, and other infrastructure in Africa for the stated purpose of opening up the continent to British trade. Since the argument for the economic benefits of expansion carried the day, projects were judged on how well they could reduce grants-in-aid and increase tax revenues.[23] Furthermore, colonial governments were expected to foot the bill for their own development projects, a situation which in turn required the imposition of new taxes and the establishment of a class of free wage labor.

In *Mister Johnson* Cary dramatizes the wage labor shortage and the local chief's collaboration with Rudbeck and Johnson in road building. Rudbeck and Johnson are collaborators of the highest order in the building of the road. Rudbeck has appropriated the road-building scheme from his D.O., but he can take it only so far. He needs Johnson's imagination. Rudbeck has the political position and the persistence necessary to see the project through; Johnson knows how to motivate people and how to create solutions to seemingly insoluble problems. Development projects demand labor as well as capital, but in the late nineteenth and early twentieth centuries such labor was largely unavailable in Africa. Until 1895 colonial policy had not produced a class of free wage labor, that is, workers willing to trade their services for money. "Colonialism," as Goran Hyden points out, "did not erase precapitalist modes of production. It did destroy the precolonial one but it generated a new precapitalist mode based on independent peasant production."[24] In effect, this meant that former subsistence farmers were now producing export crops and food for their own consumption. Land was readily available, and the use of money was limited.[25] The labor necessary for such projects as road building could only be obtained through forms of coercion and/or bribery,[26] prompting colonial government officials such as Rudbeck (and Johnson) to ally themselves with local chiefs who were the only reliable guarantors of manpower.[27] Local chiefs had coercive power to provide workers, which they were willing to use to retain their powerful positions and to obtain the money offered them by the British.

Johnson's dealings with local chiefs in the building of the Fada Road can be seen in this context of cajolery and bribery. In the nineteenth and early twentieth centuries, roads in Nigeria were designated as "native" or "political" depending on whether they were intended for the enhancement of trade or for military purposes. In both cases, roads were built and maintained by compulsory labor: "All able-bodied males between fifteen and fifty (in Southern Nigeria this applied also to women between fifteen and forty) were liable to a maximum of twenty-four days' labour each year. Failure to comply could lead to a fine of £1 or one month's imprisonment . . . "[28] Chiefs and headmen received compensation for each mile completed (10 shillings per mile in 1907), with the result that a system of cheap roads was constructed throughout Nigeria in less than two decades. George M. Foster discusses how in Nigeria, Oceana, and India local rivalries and intervillage competition led to accelerated change, especially in the construction of roads and paths.[29] Cary presents Johnson using similar free trade competition to motivate workers as well as bribes to ensure the chiefs' collaboration. The use of compulsory labor was not considered to be a problem by British colonial officials who regarded it first as a necessity for the completion of projects, second, as consistent with existing social practices, and third, as having the longer-term beneficial effect of producing the very wage labor class that is necessary for capitalist economic development.[30]

## JOYCE CARY AS DISTRICT OFFICER AND ROAD-BUILDER

Cary came to Africa 19 years after the policy shift initiated by Chamberlain which gave government the direct responsibility for infrastructure development in the colonies. Roads, ports, and railroads had been developed at government initiative in Nigeria for almost two decades by the time Cary came out to Nigeria, and their economic and civilizing roles were part of the conventional wisdom of the new imperialism. The youthful Cary eagerly accepted his part in building roads, though his enthusiasm for road building and his perception of its relationship to the British colonial mission was to evolve over the course of his six years' tenure in the Northern Nigerian Political Service. In 1914 he attended a three-month preparatory course at the Imperial Institute in London. He reports that the practical information taught was essentially useless to him in Nigeria.[31] But it is clear that Cary was immediately convinced by his training of the rightness of Lord Lugard's policy of indirect rule as the most pragmatic, least intrusive, and most effective means of governance in Nigeria. Cary eventually came to understand the difficulties of distinguishing between indirect and direct rule, but he never explicitly repudiated his belief in the goals and methods of indirect rule. As Helen Gardner reports, "[Cary] wholeheartedly accepted British colonial policy and his duty, as its instrument, to assist the process by which an old tribal society was to transform itself into modern self-governing states."[32]

Railway lines were in place when Cary arrived in Nigeria, and he rode the main line from Lagos to Zaria and thereafter a miner's line to Gurrum. At Gurrum he was met by District Officer H. S. W. Edwardes, later to become Cary's mentor and friend in Nigeria, who was a passionate believer in the betterment of peoples' lives through the laying and improvement of roads. In 1913 Edwardes had published a pamphlet, *On the Improvement of Native Paths in Northern Nigeria*, in which he defended the desirability and practicality of such projects. Cary in his role as district officer, like Rudbeck, accepted the argument and determined to follow in his mentor's steps. Edwardes is transformed into Old Sturdee, the road-building advocate, in *Mister Johnson*.

Cary was fascinated by road and bridge building during his entire stay in Nigeria. It was not until 1919, however, that he was in a position to convert his desires into action. Cary had developed a plan to link Bussa and Kaiama in Borgu, where he was district officer, with the main road running along the province's western border. He saw the connecting road as a means of situating Borgu within established trade routes, thereby producing a consequent increase in trade.[33] Included in this plan was an enhancement which his superiors refused to fund, the building of *zungos* to lodge travelers at a small fee. Cary noted two results of road building, both of which were to appear in *Mister Johnson*: trade increased, and so did crime and dislocation. As money and goods appeared in Borgu, so too did crime for which he was blamed by the local chief who resented the trouble the road caused. As Cary concluded, "What I called progress, he saw, again quite fairly, as a backward step into social confusion, crime

[and] political strife. . . ."[34] Cary continued to build roads and bridges until his departure from Nigeria in 1919, starting and leaving for completion by his district officer successor and his work foremen, Tasuki, an ambitious connecting road from Kaiama to Ilorin in the South. On learning that his replacement was soon to arrive, Cary wrote, " . . . I will be in Kontagora early in December. I am to build a bridge there which may take a day or two, but I should be able to catch a boat about the middle of December and be home early in January."[35] Bishop reports that Cary had begun new road projects which his successor would have to complete: "I shall send for a gang and start the work," declared Cary. "This is my cunning. I want my policy to go on."[36]

In *Mister Johnson*, the creative force that leads to the building of the road emanates from Clerk Johnson, not District Officer Rudbeck. The authorial voice notes that Rudbeck was born to receive inspiration rather than to give it. It is from D. O. Sturdee, the Edwardes figure, that Rudbeck receives the idea of building a road and from Johnson the inspiration for how to complete this particular major road. He absorbs ideas from Johnson without realizing their source. It is Johnson who gives him the idea of keeping the road work going by drawing on the cash reserve in anticipation of the next year's tax receipts. It is Johnson who finds beer to keep the crew contented on the road's more remote stretches. The chapters on road building in *Mister Johnson* capture the feeling Cary expressed in his own road-building efforts in Borgu: the pleasure of surveying the route, of rousing the village gangs, of watching the road stretch forth into the bush, and of contemplating the increase in trade and revenue that the road will produce. Underpinning this excitement and sense of accomplishment is a belief in the role of the road in the economic liberation of Africa. Cary rejects the cultural protectionist utterings of types like District Officer Blore and the sentimental views of Celia who romanticizes the squalor and misery of Fada. Indeed, the description of the opening of the road captures the narrator's vision of the twentieth century penetrating Borgu. As the road gangs celebrate completing the last stretch of tarmac, they hear a noise in the distance somewhere "between drumming and gunfire." The road is clearly both a promise and a threat, a source of the benefits and evils of western civilization.

Cary's imagery of the road in this novel is related to the passionate but ambivalent feelings which he experienced during his road-building in

> Borgu in 1919: " . . . this is as some Roman engineer felt when he strolled down the long reaches of Watling Street, and wondered how long he would be permitted to foretell the future of Britain . . . "[37]

When Cary has the road itself speak to Rudbeck, it is clear that the road is more than a means of transport:

> I'm smashing up the old Fada—I shall change everything and everybody in it. I am abolishing the old ways, the old ideas, the old law; I am bringing wealth and opportunity for good as well as vice, new powers to men and therefore new conflicts. I am the revolution. I am giving you plenty of trouble already, you governors, and I am going to give you plenty more. I destroy and I make new. What are you going to do about it? I am your idea.[38]

## REDISCOVERY

After 1895 Britain adopted an imperial policy which sought to develop the economies of its West African colonies through the introduction of western industrial technology. Joyce Cary's novel *Mister Johnson* provides a dramatic realization of this process. A central element of the novel is the construction of a road connecting a remote Nigerian district with the main north-south highway, thereby linking a hitherto isolated region to the outside world. The road and those who collaborate to make it a reality become technological and human "tools of empire." By opening up the Nigerian hinterlands to imperial economic designs, the road extends and strengthens the reach of the empire. By uncritically initiating the building of roads and bridges for the empire, figures such as Rudbeck serve as its agents. By providing the ideas and manipulating local tribesmen to complete the actual construction, Johnson assists the very empire which ends his life.

Critics have disagreed over what to make of the 17 year-old Nigerian clerk, Johnson. Is he the prototypical creative artist in an environment which cannot appreciate him, an instrumental character whose primary role is to assist the district officer in completing the road, or a stereotypical African created by a western author? The introduction of technology and the shift in imperial policy away from laissez faire and toward state-initiated economic development of the African colonies cast a new light on the problem of the Johnson figure in the novel. Johnson is an unintended victim of a policy shift, and, by extension, so is Nigeria.

Road building is at the center of Cary's story, and the circumstance of Johnson's death is indeed a masterful study of British imperialism. *Mister Johnson* signifies the shift in Colonial Office policy vis-a-vis African development. In dramatizing the relationship of technology to empire the novel reflects Cary's experience as road-builder and "victim" of empire. Road building was part of Chamberlain's plan for the economic development of the African colonies and a telling example of the interconnectedness of empire and technology. As a young district officer in Nigeria in 1914–19, Cary subscribed to the goals of indirect rule and believed that the building of roads and expansion of trade would lead to a more democratic and free Africa. Even toward the end of his tenure, however, Cary had some doubts about British administration in Nigeria. By 1937, when he is writing *Mister Johnson*, Cary had serious reservations about some imperial policies and the slow pace at which freedom was coming to Africa. He was less sanguine than before about the creative, liberating potential of projects such as the road and more concerned with the destructive consequences for the societies which development projects tore asunder.

Although, as Killam[39] has indicated, Cary continued to believe in Britain's role in providing educational, political, and commercial services to Africa, by 1937 Cary most certainly understood that the liberal enterprise in Africa had not worked, that the system had broken down, and that the costs to Africans had been immense. The roads and other infrastructure constructed by the British and their collaborators no doubt led to expansion of the boundaries of empire and an increase in its power, at least for a few decades. But the moral purpose, the uplifting purpose which had been the underpinning of development projects, was a failure. The road was destructive, not creative. It led to the corruption and death of many Johnsons, not to the freedom and fulfillment it promised.

By believing that Britain was chosen by Providence as the instrument of universal progress, and that what was good for the empire was good for the world, the British Empire created countless tragic stories such as Johnson's. It was a high price, and one the world is still paying today.

## REFERENCES

1. Joyce Cary, *Mister Johnson* (London: Victor Gollancz, 1939), 172.
2. Cary, 92.
3. Robert Wren, "Mister Johnson and the Complexity of *The Arrow of*

God" in *Critical Perspectives on Chinua Achebe*. Eds. C. L. Innes and Bernth Lindfors (London: Heinemann, 1978), 207.

4. Wren, 207.

5. William van O'Connor. *Joyce Cary* (New York and London: Columbia Univ. Press, 1966), 22.

6. Barbara Fisher. *Joyce Cary: The Writer and his Theme* (Gerrards Cross, England: Colin Smythe, 1980), 22–27.

7. Alan Bishop. *Joyce Cary, Gentleman Rider* (Oxford: Oxford Univ. Press, 1989), 102.

8. Michael J. C. Echeruo. *Joyce Cary and the Dimensions of Order* (Ibadan, Nigeria: Ibadan Univ. Press, 1979), 14–15. See also, Cornelia Cook, *Joyce Cary: Liberal Principles* (Barnes & Noble, 1981), 12–14.

9. Bishop, 130.

10. Daniel R. Headrick. *The Tools of Empire: Technology and European Imperialism in the Nineteenth Century* (New York and Oxford: Oxford Univ. Press, 1981), 3.

11. Headrick, 3.

12. R. A. Buchanan. *Technology and Social Progress* (Oxford: Pergamon, 1965), 123–24.

13. Buchanan, 53.

14. Ronald Robinson and John Gallagher. *Africa and the Victorians: The Climax of Imperialism in the Dark Continent* (New York: St. Martin's, 1961), 29–30.

15. Paul Kennedy. *The Rise and Fall of the Great Powers* (New York: Vintage, 1987), 153.

16. Lawrence James. *The Rise and Fall of the British Empire* (London: Abacus, 1995), 171.

17. Kennedy, 156.

18. Robinson and Gallagher, 29–30.

19. Robinson and Gallagher, 40.

20. Robinson and Gallagher, 395.

21. Cited in Robinson and Gallagher, 397.

22. Robinson and Gallagher, 397.

23. Robinson and Gallagher, 408–09.

24. Goran Hyden. *Beyond Ujamaa in Tanzania: Underdevelopment and an Uncaptured Peasantry* (London: Heinemann, 1980), 42.

25. Anne Phillips. *The Enigma of Colonialism: British Policy in West Africa* (London and Bloomington: Indiana Univ. Press, 1989), 11.

26. P. P. Rey. *Les Alliances de Classes* (Paris: Maspero, 1973) in Anne Phillips, *The Enigma of Colonialism: British Policy in West Africa* (London and Bloomington: Indiana Univ. Press, 1989), 11.

27. Phillips, 11.

28. Phillips, 40.

29. George M. Foster. *Traditional Cultures and the Impact of Technological Change* (New York: Harper & Brothers, 1962).

30. Phillips, 40–41.

31. Alan Bishop, 104.

32. Helen Gardner. "Foreword," *Joyce Cary: Selected Essays*. Ed. A. G. Bishop (London: Michael Joseph, 1976), xi.

33. Bishop, 167.

34. Joyce Cary. "Policy for Aid." *Confluence* 4, 3(1955): 292–301.
35. Quoted in Bishop, 183.
36. Quoted in Bishop, 183.
37. R. W. Noble. *Joyce Cary* (New York: Harper and Row, 1973), 33.
38. Cary, *Mister Johnson*, 215.
39. G. D. Killam. *Africa in English Fiction, 1874–1939* (Ibadan, Nigeria: Ibadan Univ. Press, 1968), 163.

# 8
# ACKNOWLEDGED TRUTHS: LORD BENTINCK AND THE ABOLITION OF SATI
## Bruce Westrate

In 1843, soon after assuming the post of governor of the Indian province of Sindh, its caustic conqueror, Charles Napier, received a delegation of Brahmins into his presence. They were agitated over Napier's declaration that, in accordance with British law, the practice of sati (widow-burning) was henceforward illegal. This, the Brahmins protested, constituted direct interference in a "custom" of their nation. The governor's reply was curt and menacingly effective:

> My nation has also a custom. When men burn women alive we hang them and confiscate their property. My carpenters shall therefore erect gibbets on which to hang all concerned when the widow is consumed. Let us all act according to our particular customs.[1]

Napier's retort serves as a metaphor for the ongoing debate which swirls around the question of empire and culture, rival perspectives looking past each other. The incident also illustrates, in stark simplicity, what can happen when deep-seated cultural mores run afoul of one another, as so often happened in the colonial setting. Even more striking was Napier's willingness to wield authority so firmly, by virtue not only of the dictates of British law, but also by those of British civilization as well, thereby arrogating unto himself a position of moral as well as political superiority. In this, of course, he exercised the conqueror's writ, timeless in its pedigree, yet discretionary in its application. Notwithstanding this, Napier's dismissive rebuke of Hindu holy men was made pursuant to an inarguably commendable objective—the preservation of human life.

The history of the British Empire is replete with similar incidents in which officials, the grand along with the nondescript, assumed the risks of exercising "cultural insensitivity" not only to promote their economic, strategic, and political interests but also to advance their perceptions of the common social or moral good. More often than not, they probably viewed these priorities as interchangeable. And while the success of these men was neither unalloyed nor impeccably consistent, it was that sort of inconsistency which usually attends the trials of imperfect experimentation. John Buchan once described the empire of which he was a part as "a strong wind freshening the stuffiness of the old lands."[2] Such observations give rise to certain queries which may be provocative, even incendiary, in the modern context. Nonetheless, he may have had a point. At the end of the day, have postcolonial deconstructionists really said all that may be said on the subject of "cultural imperialism"? Was it (is it) an entirely odious phenomenon? If so, then equally provocative questions intrude. Whence did current notions of "basic human rights," so popular as a gauge of contemporary global behavior, spring? And if international standards of human conduct have become so fungible as to render transcivilizational concepts of morality subjective, and hence meaningless, to what do today's universal moral "truths," to the extent they exist at all, owe their conception and definition?

These questions carry broad implications for the western world, and for that reason the subject of empire is particularly instructive. After all, as Edward Said has pointed out, cultural confrontation on an international scale is attributable "to the globalized process set in motion by modern imperialism."[3] It was because the British Empire was arguably the most diverse, the most multicultural in history that its administrators first experienced the agony of attempting to accommodate abstract British principles to the reality of widely divergent cultural mores and traditions among subject peoples. This task was daunting in that it demanded a calculus that factored in both profound moral questions and the prudential dictates of imperial governance. On this cutting edge of cultural confrontation were to be found many issues which still resonate loudly today: debates about justice, humanity, religious extremism, treatment of women and children, and the keeping of the peace. The empire thus remains a rich mine for inquiry and a fascinating prism through which to refract current disputes involving cultural disjunction. Occasionally they all might dovetail. More often, they did not.

The struggle of district officers, merchants, soldiers, civil servants, missionaries, and even M.P.s to reconcile the demands of conscience, practicality, and self-interest sometimes gave rise to progressive solutions through the application of "common sense." By this resort, some imperial administrators defined both the practical limits of their sufferance for exotic beliefs and practice and a sense of their own mission to uphold a minimal standard of British civilization. Lord Napier succinctly articulated this principle in his confrontation with the Brahmin holy men over sati. So, while British administrators were generally, and of necessity, solicitous of the diverse peoples over whom they had charge, they came to rule by a core conviction that upheld the superiority and beneficence of their own civilization. Occasionally and with commendable grit, they undertook to express these convictions by both word and deed, sometimes at great risk. This is not to impute an overblown rectitude to the imperial enterprise, but merely to acknowledge an unmistakable conscientiousness in British paternalism, one which belies the postmodern stereotype and reveals a substantial humanitarian and geopolitical legacy. The ubiquity of Britain's imperial bequest which remains with us today, from the abolition of slavery and sati, to representative government, universal application of law, individual liberty, tolerance of pluralism, and the English language as a common medium of expression attests both to the philosophic appeal and the judicious pragmatism of Britain's imperial method.

In adopting this course, British imperialists acted sensibly, commendably, but not perhaps as modern relativists might have done. An imperial ethos eventually emerged which was impelled by bias for British culture and a sense of mission. In the end this tutelary imperative predominated over the less attractive impulses of racism, chauvinism, and short-term self-interest to restrain the most odious manifestations of alien cultures as well as their own. More significantly, this predisposition provided a philosophical basis upon which both colonizer and colonized might grope for common ground. A secular sense of Britishness was cultivated among native western-educated elites that, in a limited but critical way, transcended what might otherwise have been insuperable cultural barriers and facilitated modernization. Many Britons realized they were sowing the seeds of future resistance and national separation. Some regarded this as an inevitable, even desirable, prospect. If the eventual result was not always the one hoped for, the fault cannot be laid altogether in the dooryard of the British nation.

The British Empire deserves no apologia. A more worthwhile goal is to buttress a philosophical correction of perspective that associates the phenomenon with some of the western world's best, rather than its worst impulses, particularly in Africa and Asia. Stains on the imperial record such as the trans-Atlantic slave trade, the "Rape of Bengal," reaction to the Indian "Mutiny," Caribbean neglect, Irish misrule, and the Amritsar Massacre are indelible, and will remain so. But to confine that context to an opprobrious indictment not merely distorts the record but also gratuitously tarnishes a decidedly progressive historical force, while at the same time embittering and alienating rightful heirs to western tradition worldwide. This is rightly "a debate which should be driven by analysis and exegesis," Brigitte Berger notes, "not multiculturalism's reliance on intuition . . . [where] everything must be expressed unequivocally and starkly."[4] The "purpose," Bernard Lewis points out

> is not to set up a moral competition—to compare castration and apartheid as offenses against humanity or to argue the relative wickedness of Eastern and Western practices, it is rather to refute the claims of both excessive virtue and exclusive vice and to point to certain common failings of our common humanity. The correction of error—even of emotionally satisfying and useful error—is a legitimate, indeed a necessary task of the historian.[5]

The deconstruction which multiculturalist critics of the British Empire employ and the cultural relativism they derive from it imply a suppleness of principle which would have seemed strange to Lord Napier. How does one, after all, morally defend the immolation of widows? The late Alan Bloom noted that "the fact that there have been different opinions about good and bad at different times, in no way proves that none is true or superior to others." Moreover, Bloom argues,

> It is important to emphasize that the lesson the students are drawing from their studies is simply untrue. History and the study of cultures do not teach or prove that values or cultures are relative. All to the contrary, that is a philosophical premise that we now bring to our study of them. This premise is unproved and dogmatically asserted for what are largely political reasons. History and culture are interpreted in the light of it, and then are said to prove the premise. . . . Herodotus was at least as aware as we are of the rich diversity of cultures. But he took that observation to be an invitation to investigate all of them to see what was good and bad about each and find out what he could learn about good and bad from them. Modern relativists take that same observation as proof that such investigation is impossible and that we must be respectful of them all. [Thus, students are deprived of] the impulse of Odysseus who, according to Dante, traveled the world to see the virtues and vices of men.[6]

Since multiculturalism's ceaseless crusade against the sins of western man goes hand-in-glove with an insistence on cultural parity, a redirected examination of the British Empire may cast light on whether such aims are either politically possible or morally desirable. Is the deconstructed nation really a viable concept? What lessons does history teach as to its prospective success, beyond claims of diversity's celebrants? Can the traditions which have sustained human progress in the western world coexist harmoniously alongside contradictory mores and principles? Was the British Empire actually the scourge of diversity so frequently portrayed? And is true multiculturalism an antidote, a prescription for openness and harmony or, absent the standard bestowed by common tradition, a blueprint for social fragmentation and incoherence? Is it the promise of felicity's motherlode or philosophical alchemy, naive and chimerical—a multiculturalist mirage giving way upon approach to some of the unfortunate traditions which the British tried to address? Perhaps the answer lies starkly before us, among the bones of the largest empire the world has ever known. Its legacy, though incessantly excoriated of late, remains at its essence strangely unrepudiated by the modern world.

In historical narratives, of course, empires come and empires go. Until relatively recently in human history, most of the globe was governed, not by neatly packaged nation-states, but by empires. To the extent that conquerors, from Alexander to Justinian to Mohammad to Akbar, cared to affect the moral evolution of subject peoples, success was limited by the context of the appeal, coming as it did from the throne of the "oppressor" and generally steeped in the tenets of a foreign faith.

Throughout its early history, the British Empire was no different. Impelled by the dictates of trade and expanding geopolitical ambitions, Britons bested their competitors in North America and India. But the East India Company's expansion in India was a private mercantilist enterprise imposed upon on an ancient, rich, but declining civilization. And while this imbalance exposed numberless openings for the opportunistic British, the sense of remorse which subsequent exploitation ultimately evoked transformed the manner in which the British came to view the people of India and themselves.

Why was this so? By the late eighteenth century, Great Britain was in the throes of the industrial revolution which, in turn, spawned cultural counterparts in Protestant evangelicalism and utilitarianism. Both phenomena sprang from impulses to compensate for the humanitarian atrocities and social dislocation attendant upon rapid industrial development. These movements fundamentally altered the manner in which social, political, and economic relationships were viewed. The impulse to reform among certain Britons of the early nineteenth century represented a synthesis between the secular energy of utilitarians who believed in the malleability of human nature and the beneficent impact of universal laws promoting the "greatest good for the greatest number" with evangelical tenets emphasizing the virtues of intense individualism, liberty, the exaltation of conscience, and faith in the sudden transformation of human character.[7] Such convictions lent reformist, messianic fervor to an already well-established concept which Orlando Patterson has dubbed the "noblest achievement of Western Civilization: the valorization of personal liberty"

> That people are free to do as they please within limits set only by the personal freedom of others; that legally persons are equal before the law; that philosophically the individual's separate existence is inviolable; that psychologically the ultimate human condition is to be liberated from all internal and external constraints in one's desire to realize one's self . . . all add up to a value complex that not only is unparalleled in any other culture but, in its profundity and power, is superior to any single complex of values conceived by mankind.[8]

More pointedly, such beliefs proved exportable to Britain's empire in India through like-minded administrators mindful of the peculations of Clive and the maladministration of Cornwallis. Introduction of the reformist zeal of the utilitarians and evangelicals into a culture about which Britain had hitherto known very little and cared even less set the stage for a clash over cultural values. While such thinkers as Jeremy Bentham and James Mill have not fared well in the historical literature of late, that verdict is by no measure unequivocal. Bentham, after all, carved his intellectual niche by "carrying the war of criticism and refutation, the conflict with falsehood and absurdity into the field of practical evils."[9] As for James Mill, one Indian scholar has recently expressed reservations about all the criticism, confessing "[i]t is not clear we are right about this." The effects of such reformers, after all, constituted

> . . . an attempt to articulate an idiom in which cultures could not only be compared and contrasted, but also criticized. It seems to me that Mill at least offered the possibility of some sort of liberating critique, which afforded the possibility of changing the way we define ourselves in order to change our practices for the better. For such a possibility to exist, sometimes we have to pretend not to have a past. Anyway, the relationship between our past and present selves is rarely clear; at any rate, our belief in some deep fact regarding our identity may not be fully justified. If Mill's *History* [*of British India*] was an exercise in philistinism it was also a

> massive exercise in disenchantment. This disenchantment was necessary in order to cut through the bolstering of identities, which could endanger the possibilities of growth and of a critique, with which a certain set of aesthetic attitudes, still very much with us today, were in profound collusion.[10]

This profound *insight* is suitable prologue to examination of an old debate calculated to pit reformist principles against a shadowy native religious rite of dubious pedigree. The debate it evoked provided the reform-minded Governor-General, Lord William Bentinck, and his westernized native allies with the perfect opportunity to clearly, unequivocally, draw that essential distinction between religious and civil authority. For the very fact of the rite itself, and the near universal horror with which other cultures viewed it, provided the ideal target for the champion's lance, a test case for a tutelary imperative the British felt compelled to pursue. The rite in question was the object of Napier's biting scorn: "sati," the practice of self-immolation performed by some higher caste Hindu women on the pyres of their deceased husbands.

## THE ISSUE

"Sati" is a Sanskrit word, roughly translating into "chaste" or "virtuous." Its origins, though ancient, are somewhat obscure. Greek writers recorded instances of sati as early as the fourth century B.C.E.[11] Some authorities trace the practice to pre-Aryan times. Others contend it was introduced by the Scythians.[12] And although not found in Vedic scripture, there apparently had been numerous attempts to introduce deliberately corrupted texts in order to legitimize the practice.[13] A truer rendering of the sanskrit is *sahamarana* (dying in company with) and is used to describe the rite itself while "sati" is employed to denote the exalted status of the sacrificed widow. The word "suttee" is most likely a European corruption but is often found in modern texts, used interchangeably with "sati."[14]

Both ethereal and worldly rewards were proffered to widows who became sati. In addition to the eternal felicity she might enjoy with her husband, a widow would be venerated, even deified for expiating family sin for three generations. But darker motivations also intruded on a woman's decision: the specter of incarnation as an animal should she refuse, or the more immediate prospect of life as a Hindu widow, consigned to poverty, chastity, and unremitting servitude.[15] To become sati would remove these perils as well as ennobling her family and elevating their social status. Meanwhile, her in-laws would be allowed not only to keep her dowry but also to relieve themselves of the burden a widow posed to the estate. Sati was a largely regional phenomenon, most popular in Bengal, Rajputana, and Vijayanagar. And though according to holy text, public coercion of widows was a "perversion of the Dharma" (established practice), involuntary sati was evident, especially among higher-caste Hindus of Bengal and Rajasthan.[16]

Most historians, including many Indians, regard sati as an abomination. R. C. Majumdar, although confessing that the widow's "grim resolve" did "extort a sort of admiration," maintained that many cases, perhaps a large majority, did not fall under this category, adding that,

> It became also almost normal practice to take good care to see that once an unfortunate widow made the fatal choice, she could not escape the cruel fate even if she wished to do so. In not a few cases, she was even drugged for the same purpose, and her body on the funeral pyre was pressed down by bamboo poles.[17]

Iqbal Singh has dubbed sati "this euphemistic jargon of piety" which "cloaked the terrible reality of what must surely be the cruelest ritual conceived by morbid religiousity."[18] "At its best," wrote Philip Woodruff, "it implied a deeply dishonourable view of a woman's part in life, and no apologist has been able to suggest why, even if a widow must die, she should die painfully."[19]

The British were not, of course, the first to condemn sati. The Mahrattas disdained it. The Moguls were appalled by it. Akbar is supposed to have ridden from Delhi to Jodhpur, quite literally to the rescue of a raja's widowed daughter. Both Jahangir and Aurangzeb flatly outlawed the practice. The Portuguese under Albuquerque prohibited it at Goa, as did the French of Chandarnagar and the Danes at Serampore.[20] The tender age of widowed brides added to the astonishment of European observers. An early English trader, Nicholas Worthington, chronicled the case of a 10-year-old who became sati in 1616. "Our agent," he wrote, "was so greeved and amazed at the undaunted resolution of the younger woman that hee said hee would never see more burnt in that fashion while hee lived." But not all widows were so resolved:

> Nowe if any one of them purpose to burne and . . . bee brought to the fyer, and there, feelinge the scorchinge heate leape out of the fyer, father and mother will take her and bynde her and throwe her into the fyer and burne her per force.[21]

On occasion, the death of a prince could prompt a holocaust. Fifteenth-century traveler, Nicolo Conti, was amazed to learn that the Raja of

Vijayanagar had designated 2,000 to 3,000 of his 12,000 wives to become sati upon his demise.[22] In 1780, 64 women burned with Raja Ajit Singh of Marwar, while in the mid-nineteenth century Suchet Singh was accompanied by 10 wives and 300 concubines into eternity.[23]

As one might expect, attempts by individual Britons to rescue doomed widows became more frequent over time, especially in light of East India Company diffidence on the issue. The legendary Job Charnock, reputed founder of Calcutta, is said to have so rescued a princess, whom he married. In 1789, M. H. Brooks, a collector at Shahabad, saved a woman from the flames but was warned by Lord Cornwallis against any future heroics.[24] In 1803 and again in 1805, 12-year-old girls were saved by British citizens. *Parliamentary Papers* record 16 instances of successful intervention in one year alone for Ghazipur.[25] In perhaps the most notorious failure chronicled, two officers of the 10th regiment observed the attempted burning of a woman by the name of Radhabayee who twice fled the conflagration, eventually leaping into the river, whereupon four individuals attempted to drown her before she was rescued by the two men. She died in a hospital the next day.[26] Grisly alternatives were occasionally employed in the rite. The Jagi sect of East Bengal preferred burying women alive. In 1812, a 16-year-old girl was interred in a six-foot grave alongside her husband's corpse, while her parents looked on. What seemed even worse to Europeans in India, the act took place just 20 miles from Calcutta and was sanctified by the Hindu law offices of the Provincial Court of Appeal for Dacca.[27] A police superintendent in lower Bengal despaired that resistance in such circumstances was generally futile as "the people will not be disappointed of their show and the entire population of a village will turn out to assist in dragging her to the bank of the river, and keeping her on the pile."[28]

The East India Company, though professing horror at these accounts, clung tenaciously to a rigid policy of noninterference in such matters. Indeed, as a later defender would point out, to have done otherwise "would have been downright insanity in an association whose object was to do business with Indians." The British, of course, had much more at stake financially than the French or the Dutch or the Portuguese. A strict monopoly on commercial enterprise, he averred, necessitated the encouragement of "free trade and unlimited speculation in religion."[29]

By turns, however, company higher-ups came under intense pressure (which eventually reached Parliament) from missionaries and from their own officials in the hinterland of Bengal who felt that sati should be, if not suppressed outright, then at least made more difficult.[30] C. M. Lushington wrote from Trichinopoly in 1819 that the rite was tolerated "to the disgrace of the British Government" and "even abominated by the better sort of natives themselves and nowhere is it enjoined by Hindu law . . . "[31] Edmund Malony, acting magistrate in Burdwan, insisted that "enactment of such a (abolition) law is dictated by every principle of humanity . . . "[32] It is worth reiterating that, while Brahminical institutions sanctified sati, the rite was not widely practiced throughout India. Nor was it associated with the mass of middle and lower castes. Early on, company officials in the countryside recognized sati's limited scope and caste appeal, a fact which may have emboldened them. But, the frequency of their intervention into what many Hindus still deemed a sacred practice also provides a fine example of what Clive Dewey has dubbed "heroic individuals exercising free will";[33] a hundred stories of conscious decisions to prevent gross injustice despite "risks taken of stirring up riots and losing life, risks of incurring rebuke for exceeding authority."[34]

Yet for those in Parliament advancing timorously into the enterprise of governing India, there was only bad precedent. Robert Clive and Warren Hastings, stinging from Burkean rebuke, had been loathe to interfere in the religious lives of native communities.[35] They correctly discerned the nature of Hindu sensibilities on the matter and were not eager to follow the Portuguese example, given *their* unpopularity with many Indians. British rule was, as yet, too insecure in the official mind to run the risk of massive Hindu backlash. "Nothing but apprehension of evils infinitely greater than those arising from the existence of the practice," Lord Amherst explained in 1824, "should induce us to tolerate it for a single day."[36] Speaking of those infinitely greater "evils," of course, was a veiled reference to worries about security. Never very distant from the minds of governors-general as well as provincial governors was the memory of the bloody mutinies at Vellore in 1806 which erupted over issues of caste violation and cost the British over one hundred lives. "I will hope to have credit for being acutely sensible to such an outrage against humanity," the Marquis of Hastings began,

> At the same time I was aware how much danger might attend the endeavoring to suppress forcibly a practice so rooted in the religious belief of the natives. No men of low caste are admitted into the ranks of the Bengal Army. Therefore the whole of that formidable body must be regarded as blindly partial to a custom which they consider equally referable to family honour and to points of faith. To attempt the extinction of the horrid su-

perstition without being supported in the procedure by a real concurrence on the part of the army would be distinctly perilous.[37]

Only the grandiloquent Wellesley, among the early rulers of British India, felt confident enough to disdain caution in such matters. He had already forbidden Indian women from flinging their female infants into the Ganges at Saugor when he heard of the rescue from the funeral pyre of a drugged 12-year-old widow by the magistrate of Bihar. The governor-general promptly solicited the learned opinion of the *Nizámat Adálat*, the highest court of appeal under the Company's system, for advice from the resident pandits as to Hindu law in the matter as well as on prospective changes in British policy. Although Wellesley would depart India before those recommendations were returned, his frame of mind portended a shift of policy. Government maxims "to consult the opinions, customs and prejudices of the natives were fundamental," he pledged, "but only when they were consistent with the principles of humanity, morality and reason."[38]

In that spirit, policy changes derived from the recommendations of the *Nizámat Adálat* were promulgated in 1813. The shastras, they concluded, forbade sati if the widow was intoxicated, restrained or otherwise unwilling, pregnant, menstruating, below the age of 16 or pre-pubescent. Accordingly, magistrates and native police officers were instructed to attend sati ceremonies both to ascertain volition and enforce the above proscriptions. They then were to observe the ceremony so as to ensure against violations. The directives were translated into Bengali, Hindi, and Urdu.[39] Sadly, however, these measures only made a bad situation worse. Whether heightened vigilance simply yielded greater awareness of the extent of the problem or whether the fig-leaf of government regulation lent a sense of official imprimatur among the people in the countryside, is unclear.[40] What is evident is the raw statistical explosion in the number of women consigned to the flames. In the Bengal Presidency alone, the grim toll mounted: 1815 (378), 1816 (442), 1817 (707), 1818 (839).[41] Hoping to discover a solution short of outright abolition, the government, in 1817, imposed further restrictions on the custom, protecting: (1) widows with a suckling infant or child under the age of four; (2) widows with children five to seven years of age with no one to care for them; (3) women who were with their husbands at time of death but neglected to perform the rite immediately. The new regulations also forbade restraints of any kind such as cords or bamboo poles.[42] But enforcement was capricious and often token (such as ten rupee fines), and native policemen sometimes complicit. In 1817, satis were recorded of 10- and 12-year-olds, and of an 18-year-old with a 6-day-old child. In one case, sati of a pregnant widow who left behind three children brought a 12 rupee fine.[43] By the early 1820s, officially approved sati had become a perfunctory horror, bloodlessly entered into the official record:

| | |
|---|---|
| Name: | Boodul, Age 25, caste Chuttry |
| Date of Burning: | 4 August 1822 |
| Remarks: | The woman burnt along with the corpse of her husband. They had only one child, a girl of 13 years old, well provided for and she was not pregnant . . . police officers were present and I myself saw and spoke to her for a few hours before the sacrifice. There was no legal impediment to her being burnt.[44] |

Dissatisfaction with government's stance in the matter of sati was clearly building. The regulations, it seemed to many, had only made "The British Government by specific permission of the suttee, an ostensible party to the sacrifice." The company's court of directors went even further, adding: "We are averse also to the practice of making British courts expounders and vindicators of the Hindu religion when it leads to acts which not less as legislators than as Christians we abominate."[45]

Cautious Britons, agonizing over the possible consequences of abolition, held out an alternative remedy. They placed much faith in nascent western education in India. Among these was the departing Governor-General Lord Amherst who, in 1827, clearly voiced his preference for the gradual transformation of India's intellectual climate as an antidote to atavistic horrors such as sati. There were "sure means," he noted, "of bringing this barbarous custom into desuetude; and I would rather wait a few years for the gradual consummation of this desirable event."[46] Other administrators on the subcontinent, however, harbored grander visions for the impact of western education than the simple abolition of sati. Progressive proconsuls such as Mountstuart Elphinstone in Bombay, though leery of reformist zealots, went so far as to anticipate the eventual withdrawal of British power. "The most honourable death for us to die of," he mused, "should be the improvement of the natives reaching such a pitch as would render it impossible for a foreign nation to retain the government . . . " adding,

> A time of separation must come; and it is for our interest to have an early separation from a civilised people rather than a rupture with a barbarous nation, in which it is possible that all our settlers and even our commerce

would perish, along with all the institutions we had introduced into the country.[47]

More to the point, Elphinstone, while also wary of Indian response, saw an opportunity in the debate over sati to strike at the core Brahminical dogma and civilizational torpor which were so inimical to progress. The weapon of choice against Indian resistance to western influence would be education—western education. "If there be a wish to contribute to the abolition of the horrors of self-immolation," he wrote in 1824, "and ultimately to the destruction of superstition in India, it is scarcely necessary now to prove that the only means of success lies in the diffusion of knowledge." Education, he felt, might prove so efficacious as to obviate radical measures on issues such as sati. British vulnerability, although dictating caution in religious matters, "requires the adoption of some measure to counteract them, and the only one is, to remove their prejudices and to communicate our own principles and opinions by this diffusion of national education."[48] This prescription, of course, begged the probable question of eventual independence, and like Elphinstone, Madras Governor Thomas Munro looked on that prospect as "no cause of despair." Citing the mysterious dynamism impelling the rise and decline of history's myriad civilizations, he saw change as inexorable, having no doubt that "we shall in time so far improve the character of our Indian subjects as to enable them to govern and protect themselves."[49] The stakes in the impending debate over sati had grown higher than even the lives of several thousand widows might suggest. Precedents would be set which were to cast long shadows on British rule in India. If sati were outlawed, it would mark the first instance "of an exercise of state authority for the purpose of prohibiting anti-social customs."[50] More pointedly, "in doing so the British Government were in effect deciding whether to accept Hindu standards of value for India or to denounce them, at least in this respect, as barbarous."[51]

British policy makers in Calcutta and in London pondering the imponderable, were still cautious, even timorous; while knowing a crime when they saw one, they were chary of becoming indistinguishable from evangelicals whose denunciation of sati seemed to them hysterical. Mucking around in the arcana of exotic religious faiths was tricky business. But the British were both principled and practical. The philosophical dilemma which vexed David Hume: that of how to infer virtue (what ought to be) from a fact (what is) was also the question that had to be answered before the British could justify the risk among themselves. It proved necessary to strike a philosophic balance between prudent self-interest and what James Q. Wilson calls the "moral sense," that which they intuited to be "right" or "wrong" based on their conceptions of the minimal requirements of a just society.[52] This critical result, while a perspective usually ignored or disdained by philosophers, was the basis of Clive Dewey's much maligned "'common sense,' the last refuge of the pragmatist, as low-grade ideology: a rag bag of rules of thumb, culled from forgotten thinkers."[53] Professor Eric Stokes, characterized this mentality as a "practical cast of mind."[54] With this attribute, many of Britain's "men on the spot" in India were generously endowed. One prominent biographer of the nineteenth century, while acknowledging the difficulty of codifying the limits of toleration and incitements to intervene in religious matters, noted:

> But practical administrators should never have any difficulty in deciding when a Hindu practice must be considered a foul stain on British rule. It is unjustifiable to take steps which point to our desire to convert the Hindus . . . But respect and protection . . . must not allow us to be blind to acts which are in contravention of all religion, and opposed to the most clearly established rights of humanity. No religion can justify the sacrifice of innocent persons. A civilised Government is bound to protect them or lose its reputation.[55]

The sati question was so crucial because it contained within it element both of profound opportunity and of peril. Like other, more popular reforms such as the suppression of the Thugs, abolition clearly had humanitarian appeal. Yet, whereas the Indian public at large condemned Thuggee, "those who performed sati were held up as model wives and as paragons of virtue."[56] This reform would take place not in accord with public sentiment, but in the teeth of it. What was really needed was a bold reformer, one capable of formally codifying and explicating "common sense" in such a way that India's secular state might buttress principles of western law. The goal was to make Hindu India accessible to western reason, *not* to eviscerate its spiritual core. That fateful executor arrived in 1828.

## Bentinck

William Cavendish Bentinck, born in 1774, was a scion of the Whig aristocracy, second son of a prime minister, the Duke of Portland. After entering the Coldstream Guards in 1791, he obtained a captaincy in the 2nd Light Dragoons, participating in the 1794 campaign in Flanders as an aide to the Duke of York. Following a stint in the

West Indies, Bentinck was selected to serve as England's military representative to Marshal Suvorov in Northern Italy and Switzerland, later transferring to the Austrian army in that same capacity until 1801. Traveling next to Egypt, young Bentinck gained a cavalry command under Sir Ralph Abercromby. Returning to England in 1803, he married Lady Mary Acheson and three months later was notified of his nomination by the East India Company to the governorship of Madras Presidency, the youngest governor ever sent to Indian shores.[57]

It was during his tenure at Fort St. George, Madras, that the Vellore mutinies occurred over the issue of a new style of turban (with leather cockade) and a prohibition against the wearing of caste marks. It was a bloody but brief affair, suppressed with swift, remorseless energy. Bentinck withdrew the offending orders as to dress, and the ranks were pacified. Sir Thomas Munro ventured the opinion that the turban issue was a serious one, seen by the sepoys as part of a scheme for their forcible conversion. The court of directors declared that the Vellore affair had "impaired our confidence" in the governor, and Bentinck was recalled.[58] This was mortifying to him. He felt wounded by the censure as he had actually "reestablished order and confidence" and "averted the numerous calamities which the adoption of an opposite system of policy would have entailed on India."[59] After extensive service with Arthur Wellesley in Spain and as military governor of Sicily and Mediterranean commander-in-chief, Bentinck returned to England and entered Parliament for Lynn. In 1819, he was once again offered his old post at Madras, but, having failed to receive adequate reparation for his earlier dismissal, declined. Vindication was to come eight years later in the offer of the governor-general's post, as successor to Lord Amherst.

Prior to his departure in 1827, Bentinck was feted at the house of radical imperialist George Grote, where he reportedly sipped "the pure milk of the Benthamite word" that would guide him in the remaining years of his career in India.[60] He set sail "with a battle cry ringing in his ears"[61]

> to secure and improve the condition of all classes, to bring into life the vast dormant resources which undoubtedly exist and to found a British Empire in India not less worthy of admiration by all Asiatic nations than Britain has been to the European world.[62]

Bentinck had notions of nation-building on his mind, intent on using western knowledge transmitted through the media of English and vernacular tongues, rather than the traditional classical languages of

Sanskrit, Arabic, and Persian, the study of which for Indians he regarded as a "time-wasting nuisance."[63] The governor-general would prove a valuable patron of western education and vernacular instruction, publishing grammar guides and dictionaries in those tongues which he considered "the languages of the country."[64] He reformed Fort William College to train young officials in these vernaculars, while personally studying Leyden's works in Persian and Arabic. "General education," Bentinck wrote, "is my panacea for the regeneration of India" as "the ground must be prepared and the jungle cleared away before the human mind can receive with any prospect of real benefit, the seeds of improvement."[65] He also ended flogging in the Indian army.

Calcutta society hardly knew what to make of Bentinck, with his taciturnity, his fondness for the natives, his "simple tastes, sober dress and Christian propriety." Indeed, imperial grandees found his modesty and pacifism rather dull. Notwithstanding Bentinck's lack of charisma, Moorhouse reminds us, "morality hallmarked everything he did in the next seven years."[66]

The issue of widow-burning was quickly to command center stage in Bentinck's administration. The religious tenets which underlay the practice epitomized that "jungle" he hoped so fervently to clear away from the Hindu psyche. Up to now, Bentinck felt, British rule had been "cold, selfish and unfeeling," deficiencies he was determined to correct.[67] So it was the issue of sati that the new governor-general would select to force the showdown with Brahminical India and, again, that choice was not capricious. It was this practice which aroused Europeans; company officials and missionaries had long been pressing for abolition. Moreover, half measures had clearly proved ineffective. Besides, the rite stood as a glaring affront to British notions of humanity and justice. But the issue also held great promise as a herald of impending westernization. Sati, Bentinck had been informed, was in all probability scripturally illegitimate and by no means universally practiced. Yet since the Brahmin priesthood persisted in defending it, an opportunity impended, rhetorically and culturally, to diminish clear obstacles to his designs. Even more fortunate for Bentinck, he had allies within the Indian intelligentsia, scholars educated in English who shared the governor-general's disgust with sati if not his timetable or his tactics. This cohort was led by the legendary founder of the Brahmo Samaj, Rammohun Roy. With these advantages at his command, Bentinck saw little sense in maintaining strict traditional neutrality in religious matters, if British rule were to mean anything more than simply brute force or ledger entries. For India to be drawn into the comity of nations "criteria other than those emerging from Indian society itself would have to be applied."[68] In retrospect, the "moral sense" may have provided Lord Bentinck with both philosophical justification and considerable optimism concerning India's future. As Wilson has noted

> The strength of the moral senses are revealed when circumstances permit their fuller expression and wider effect. In the new order, hardly anyone wished to return to a life in which the customs required suttee, infanticide, infibulation, cannibalism or ritual torture.[69]

Still, Lord William was careful to prepare the ground before proceeding with outright abolition. He solicited and received an updated report from the *Nizámat Adálat*, recording its strong opinion that sati was clearly an undesirable practice and might be safely prohibited. Preoccupied with the security question, the governor-general canvassed the opinions of 49 police superintendents throughout Bengal. The results were heartening. Five opposed any interference whatever. Twelve were favorably inclined toward abolition, but preferred more indirect, less absolute, means. Eight supported abolition through the indirect interference of local magistrates, such as had already been tried. Twenty-four of the officers advocated complete, total, and immediate public suppression of the practice. Almost unanimously, they also minimized the measure's probable impact on the ranks of the sepoy army, which apparently cared less about the issue than hitherto supposed. Sati was virtually unknown in the ranks, they pointed out and "any interest the sepoy felt in the matter must be indirect and probably remote."[70]

Meanwhile, R. M. Roy who had long been at the forefront of a movement from the Indian side against sati, weighed in with his assessment. Roy felt strongly that pure Hinduism, which he regarded as a form of Deism, forbade altogether such "sinful" rites.[71] He fully realized, moreover, the significance of British reform in the larger Indian context. The arrival of the English, stressed Roy, offered the promise of freedom from "the long continuing tyranny of its former rulers" under the tutelage of "a nation who are not only blessed with the enjoyment of civil and national liberty, but also interest themselves in promoting liberty and social happiness . . . among those nations to which their influence extends." Further,

> Finding them [the British] generally more steady and moderate in their conduct, I gave up my prejudices against them and became inclined in their favour feeling persuaded that their rule, though a foreign yoke, would

lead most speedily and surely to the amelioration of the native inhabitants.[72]

Yet despite his conviction that British rule would eventually result in India's "improvement, both moral and social," Roy had qualms about government's abandoning professed religious neutrality as their first act after "having obtained the supremacy . . . " This prompted the inevitable comparisons to "the Mohammedan conquerors attempting to force upon us their own religion."[73] Instead, Roy wished to avoid the general apprehension which prohibition might incite, by suppressing the practice quietly, unobservedly strengthening legal obstacles through the indirect agency of the police. Indeed, Roy himself intervened on numerous occasions; his gentle, cerebral rebukes often eliciting contempt from the assembled multitudes. Roy's confidante and cofounder of the Brahmo Samaj, Dwarkanath Tagore (grandfather of Rabindranath) was passionately opposed to the practice as well, regarding it as an impediment to India's claim to civilization. Like most Bengalis of that era who were in daily contact with Europeans, he regarded sati as "personally embarrassing."[74]

While Roy and the Brahmo Samaj labored to persuade their countrymen to voluntarily abandon sati, Bentinck took heart. Such compelling allies, in spirit if not in method, appeared to vindicate his reading of Indian prospects. Roy also saw the issue, as did Bentinck, in civilizational context, anticipating liberation "from cruel murder under the cloak of religion, and our character, as a people, [rescued] from the contempt and pity with which it has been regarded, on account of this custom, by all civilized nations on the surface of the globe."[75] In hindsight, as V. S. Naipaul has pointed out, such men seem extraordinarily courageous. Given the ubiquity of western influences today, "simple people everywhere have to make some accommodation to the civilization that encircles and attracts them." However, "In the static conditions of Indian civilization at the time—with all its pressures towards old ways, old virtues—it required exceptional intellectual power to recognize the new gifts of Europe."[78] Such allies Bentinck was loathe to squander. The time seemed right for dramatic action, and if the likes of Roy did not agree on the timing, they might yet be brought round, perhaps with a *fait accompli*. That would force the issue by compelling a small but increasingly incandescent, westernized elite to confront the paradox posed by Britain's tutelary imperative. This was a puzzle for political philosophers attempting to straddle the issue "who approved of national independence and disapproved of pushing widows into the fire."[77]

## THE MINUTE

Lord Bentinck's Minute on sati, issued on 8th November, 1829, is a masterpiece of reasoned, judicious argument. He opens by defining the issue, as one might expect, in the broadest possible context, encompassing the future prospects of British India by juxtaposing the "horror" of the "consignment year after year of hundreds of innocent victims to a cruel and untimely end" against the peril posed to the safety of the British Empire in India, including risks to "those great improvements—affecting the condition not of hundreds and thousands but of millions—which . . . in the light of humanity itself may be considered as a still greater evil." Irrespective of the baser impulses which gave rise to Britain's Indian empire, Bentinck now seemed determined to redefine those impulses. The only consideration which might be defensible in tolerating sati was, within the governor-general's Olympian framework, "the good of mankind."[78]

Bentinck then delineates the sources of his reformist zeal, the wellsprings of evangelical and utilitarian principle, sufficiently secularized in tone to deflect suspicion that he might be proselytizing, yet not so much as to sever the humanitarian link between impulses of evangelicalism and reason. "On the one side, Religion, Humanity, under the most appalling form, as well as vanity and ambition—in short, all the most powerful influences over the human heart—are arrayed to bias and mislead the judgment." Yet, he insists, in his departure from the dictates of religious neutrality, "nothing has been yielded to feeling, but that reason and reason alone has governed the decision."[79] And after enumerating the prudent concerns of his predecessors, he confesses that

> I should be guilty of little short of the crime of multiplied murder if I could hesitate in the performance of this solemn obligation. I have been already stung with this feeling. Every day's delay adds a victim to the dreadful list . . . [80]

In the light of Bentinck's calamitous experience in Madras over twenty years before, later passages in the Minute seem astonishingly bold. In a bow to R. M. Roy's gradualist prescriptions, he allows that sati might be suppressed by "influence and power beyond the law," which might well achieve extinction of the rite, "by a tacit sanction alone on the part of the Government." Such a course had much to recommend it. A "tacit" policy of moral suasion and indirect obstruction would avoid exciting alarm and, in addition, would be easier to retreat from in the event of violent backlash (such as at Vellore) without "any compromise of character." Yet this tack, Bentinck stresses could not be made compatible with the rule of law, especially since security concerns were now allayed. Drawing a direct and unequivocal connection between principle and power, he wrote,

> now that we are supreme, my opinion is decidedly in favour of an open, avowed, and general prohibition, resting altogether upon the moral goodness of the act and our power to enforce it.[81]

His perception of British power in India, he felt, was justified by the passive disposition of Bengalis and the natural allies created by the British among rich landed proprietors created by Permanent Settlement, despite its having been "a failure in many other respects and in its most important essentials."[82] Besides, there were many piecemeal examples of successful sati prohibition or prevention already: within the city of Calcutta; under Sir Charles Metcalfe in Delhi territory; and in Jessore where the frequency had been much lessened. These facts augured well for the prospect of general prohibition, as did the favorable verdict of the *Nizámat Adálat*. The one concession which Bentinck made to Cassandra was in the implementation of the edict, by which the police would warn participants, stay to observe, and file a report which would become the basis for subsequent prosecution. This he thought prudent, lest open confrontation court "affray or . . . acts of violence."[83]

It is in the concluding paragraphs, that the governor-general draws together themes of humanity, secular authority, future westernization, and British supremacy as keys to the significance of the prohibition. The "first step" toward the "improvement of their [Hindus] future condition as the establishment of a purer morality . . . will be dissociation of religious belief and practice from blood and murder." The promise of future advance glimmered over the horizon:

> They will then, when no longer under this brutalising excitement, view with more calmness acknowledged truths. They will see that there can be no inconsistency in the ways of Providence, that to the command received as divine by all races of men, 'No innocent blood shall be spilt,' there can be no exception; and when they shall have been convinced of the error of this first and most criminal of all their customs, may it not be hoped that others, which stand in the way of their improvement, may likewise pass away, and that thus emancipated from those chains and shackles upon their minds and actions, they may no longer continue, as they have done, the slaves of every foreign conqueror, but that they may assume their first places among the families of mankind.[84]

In a stroke, Lord Bentinck drew an unambiguous causal connection between future westernization and the furtherance of certain universal principles ("acknowledged truths") long inherent in British legal and religious tradition, couched in terms deft enough not to alienate sympathetic Indian allies. Of course, his predecessors had taken tentative steps in this direction with the suppression of Thugee and prohibition of female infanticide. But the former could be justified as a law-and-order measure alone, while the latter, until now, was episodic and limited in its effectiveness. The abolition of sati would prove a watershed, a vital precursor to the more sweeping reforms in education and law a few years distant. This measure represented the "first important case of deviation from the Company's established policy" impelled by "a new spirit of moral earnestness—a missionary spirit in the truest sense."[85] Although Bentinck was not compelled to act by evangelical pressure and, indeed, labored to link his sati proclamation to utilitarian reason, not religion, missionary activity spanning three decades had helped provide a salutary political environment both in India and England. Thus missionaries played a significant, albeit indirect, role "in changing the temper of the age."[86] On the very day the governor-general's Minute on Sati was issued Baptist missionary William Carey rejoiced that "for the first time the Ganges flowed unblooded to the sea."[87]

Sati was now officially prohibited. Since record keeping began in 1815 and until 1829, 7,419 widows of whom the British were aware had been burned to death in Bengal alone.[88] The numbers in Rajputana were undoubtedly much higher. The practice would persist in some of the princely states through mid-century despite British lobbying against it. "When suttee has occurred in an independent state," Lord Dalhousie later wrote, "no opportunity of remonstrating has been lost."[89] Still, general abolition would take time. Eighty-four women died with Ajit Singh of Jodhpur, 14 with the Raja of Idar (seven queens, two concubines, four female slaves and a personal manservant).[90] And widow-burning would persist in Punjab until the British conquest.[91] On June 27, 1839, an Englishwoman, Miss Eden, witnessed the immolation of Ranjit Singh's harem. "Those poor dear ranees," she later recorded, "whom we visited and thought so beautiful and so merry, have actually burnt themselves . . . they were such gay young creatures, and they died with the most obstinate courage."[92] Relatedly, the widow's motivation to become sati was lessened somewhat in 1856 by Lord Dalhousie's passage of the widow's remarriage act (by which Hindu religious proscriptions were lifted), as well as by later measures dealing with child marriage and inheritance law.

For Bentinck, the results were gratifying. There was little serious resistance to the measure. On January 14, 1830, a delegation from the Brahmin elite of Calcutta presented a petition (with 800 signatures) to the government protesting abolition of "such a vital aspect of Hinduism," Bentinck's deviation from established company policy, as well as the cultural intolerance inherent in the measure.[93] Sati, the petition complained, had been misrepresented, for it was not "merely a sacred duty but a high privilege to her who sincerely believes in the doctrine of her religion . . . "[94] Bentinck rejected that argument out of hand as did his superiors in London. Tersely, Lord Lansdowne remonstrated that "every human mind must rejoice at the abolition of such a custom" and then laid the petition on the table.[95] The following year, Hindu opponents organized the Dharma Sabha in order to rally traditional defenders of sati. The governor-general was also proved right about R. M. Roy, who dispatched a congratulatory missive to him, signed by nearly 300 Hindu residents of Calcutta, which read in part as follows:

> In consideration of circumstances so disgraceful in themselves, and so incompatible with the principles of British rule, your Lordship in council, fully impressed with the duties required of you by justice and humanity has deemed it incumbent on you . . . to come to the resolution that the lives of your female Hindoo subjects should be henceforth more efficiently protected; that the heinous sin of males and females may no longer be committed, and that the most ancient and purest system of Hindoo religion should not any longer be set at nought by the Hindoos themselves.[96]

Bentinck was quick to reply:

> I trust that the reproach (of sati) is removed for ever; and feel a sincere pleasure in thinking that the Hindoos will thereby be exalted in the estimation of mankind, to an extent in some degree proportioned to the repugnance which was felt for the usage which has now ceased.[97]

"The father of modern India," as Roy is commonly known to history, had therefore rendered a verdict on Bentinck's policy as "ex-ante objection but ex-post approbation."[98] And with that reply, the governor-general had once more pressed home the point that far from desiring to extirpate Hinduism, he wished to "exalt" it though the inculcation of reason. An official British contemporary, Sir Charles Metcalfe praised the measure as "the best act performed by the British government in India."[98] However, a well-known English writer on the abolition question saw more personal than civilizational triumph in the act. "The abolition of suttee," Edward Thompson later wrote, "so far from being . . . an example of our greatness as a nation and an empire, is an example of our timidity . . . the credit is almost entirely personal, and it is Bentinck's."[100] Wilson was half-right, for the governor-general's rationale for interference was rooted in emergent

British philosophies. In any case, the new 'Regulation XVII' represented a sea change in British governance of the Indian subcontinent.

## DECONSTRUCTING BENTINCK

Notwithstanding the fulsome praise, however, Bentinck had and continues to have critics both of the perceived hubris displayed by his act and of its "darker" motives. There had, of course, always been a few apologists for sati within the British community of orientalists in India. Colonel Stewart, a member of the Asiatic Society, once gushed that it was "the most complete and ample system of moral Allegory that the world has ever produced."[101] John Zephaniah Howell, the reputed embellisher of the "Black Hole of Calcutta" tale, also looked on widow-burning as laudable, born of "heroic, as well as rational and pious principles."[102] Yet such sentiments were exceptional, even eccentric, within the British community.

Today, by contrast, such views are not so uncommon, especially issuing from some Indian and western deconstructionists and feminist scholars. Such writers have tended to deal with manifest yet inconvenient cultural disjunctions by denying the inconvenience that such overweening notions as "principles of humanity" impute. In other words, the reason westerners were horrified by sati is that they were westerners, not that there was a horror. The sati question provides insight into such issues because perspectives are bifurcated. The evolution of British Indian culture, as another historian has pointed out, is dominated by British ideas and these ideas simmer beneath the protests of those who are in revolt against "foreign ideas" for "nothing is foreign which is found in the bed-rock of human nature."[103]

Few Indian scholars defend widow-burning on its merits (such silliness is the preserve, largely of westerners). But a new generation has risen to the challenge with relativist counterattacks against western womanhood as "unchaste and therefore incapable of understanding a rite such as sati."[104] Swami Vivekananda had pioneered this route earlier, asserting that "the girls of India would die if they, like American girls, were obliged to expose half their bodies to the vulgar gaze of young men."[105] Others defend absolutely the propriety of cultural pride, even its admittedly abhorrent manifestations:

> If Englishmen can feel pride in their ancestors who grabbed one-fourth of the world's surface and not be held up to ridicule or rebuke, there is no reason why poor Indians cannot express admiration for the sacrifices

> which their women made in the past, though they may condemn the institution itself which demanded such terrible sacrifice and suffering.[106]

This is, of course, counterintuitive. There exists the very best reason to continue to hold this custom in disrepute: it still exists beneath the surface of rural India, (especially in Rajasthan), occasionally adding to Bentinck's "dreadful list."

On September 4, 1987, in the prosperous village of Deorella about 50 kilometers from Jaipur, a teenage girl named Roop Kanwar was burnt to death on the pyre of her dead husband, Maan Singh. Four thousand people witnessed the event. There were no initial reports of coercion. An "ethereal smile" reportedly graced the widow's face as the fire was lit, according to witnesses, miraculously, by divine flame. However, other witnesses heard her cry "Papa! Papa!" before the flames enveloped her. Everyone but Roop Kanwar, it seems, had a vested interest in the outcome. Her father promptly declared his daughter a martyr, thereby greatly enhancing his family's social standing. Her in-laws, though allowed to retain her dowry, now had no debased widow to support. And the entire village stood to cash in on the hordes of pilgrims habitually drawn to new martyrs and shrines (up to 10,000 a day). One of those villagers clearly summarized the widow's dilemma, remarking:

> after all, she had no life to look forward to. A widow cannot remarry in our community and she had no children. Our society treats a widow as an evil omen and an economic liability. She has to remain barefoot, sleep on the floor and can never go out of the house, for she is slandered if seen talking to a man. She is better off dead.[107]

The incident was a *cause celebre* for Indian feminists, who recognized correctly that sati was merely the most grisly manifestation of Hindu mistreatment of women, especially widows; "social prejudices . . . (which) . . . continue to dominate our life," according to one observer, "manifest fully in bride-burning and widow-burning."[108] Philip Mason, citing other modern sati accounts, earlier alleged the practice "is still there deep in the subconscious mind of a continent."[109]

Cultural issues such as those raised by sati are the shoals upon which multiculturalists founder. Because of their very nature, practices that, largely due to western influences, lack wide moral currency—sati, child marriage, female infanticide—are impossible to ignore and extremely difficult to rationalize, although determined academics futilly persist in trying. Latter day apologists-cum-cultural "protectors" apotheosize the sacrificial widow as a heroic symbol of "a devoted wife."[110] Some modern feminists likewise shrink from "invidious" comparisons of cultures. "The difference," asserts Hanne Georgeson, "between Hindu and British women was not so much the gap in their respective societies' treatment of women, but rather the fact that there was an omission of discussion about Bengali women in the British and Bengali concern for the status of women in Hindu society."[111] Though reluctantly, grudgingly, western feminist scholars deconstructing empire have conceded the efficacy of Bentinck's Regulation XVII, they have given little other credit to the British, who drew attention not only to the sati issue but also to a whole host of critical questions affecting women such as widow remarriage, inheritance laws, female infanticide, and age of consent. Georgeson construes British endeavors to assay the extent of the sati problem in 1815 as efforts at intrusive British East India Company [*sic*] "surveillance" of the lives of the people; a plot by company "watch dogs out tabling information to be able to support future policies . . . surveillance justified through the maintenance of widow-burnings" performed according to prescribed regulations.[112] Moreover, enhanced security and the use of widow-burning "as a symbol in a climate of changing ideas"[113] somehow are supposed to vitiate any more heroic portrayal of Britain's role in abolition. Sati discourses were, anyhow, chiefly concerned "with the maintenance of power and position in Bengal both for the British and sundry allied elites."[114] In that spirit, critics have gone to great lengths to impugn British motivation. William Sleeman, a renowned officer in the company service did his best to prevent a sati in 1829, pleading at length with the widow and her family, threatening reprisal with legal sanctions and criminal prosecution. This was the same Sleeman who achieved such acclaim in the campaign to suppress Thugee. His efforts were unavailing, for the widow was determined to end her life in the manner prescribed by custom. Yet latter-day cynics such as Nancy Paxton deride Sleeman for his account which apparently alluded once too often to the widow's body in describing her sati and for the "moral detachment" with which he described the act. Thus:

> Sleeman enacts the prerogative of the male colonizer as lawgiver and historian by describing how his word, his desire is written over the heads of his subjects. The relationship between body and word in this text thus helps to reveal the central place of gender in the emerging reformist political ideology. Sleeman articulates the pedagogy that justified the first formal interventions in Indian culture in order to eradicate certain 'dreadful' practices such as sati.[115]

Efforts to ban sati, therefore, are reduced to a primordial male compulsion to dominate rather than to such diversionary notions as humanity, justice, or reason.

Both Georgeson and Dorothy Stein also seek to derail the cultural question by redirecting attention to the treatment of contemporary women in English society, comparing the desperate situation of high-caste Hindu widows with the plight of bored English governesses nursing poor marriage prospects. However inapt the analogy, they grudgingly concede that

> Western ideas and religious pluralism were by and large successful in substituting less extreme, or at least less spectacular, trials for widows than the ambiguous apotheosis of sati.[116]

Thus, are the British damned with faint praise. Georgeson's and Stein's perspective conveniently ignores the documented continuum of British effort to ameliorate the condition of women in Hindu India. John Leonard reminds us that "the bad news is that all the ancient civilizations were based on gold and slaves."[117] Yet the British Empire's image in world history suffers from the signal disability of being judged so uniquely, not by the efficacy or desirability of its works, but by the purity of its heart.

Perhaps the most Olympian perch of deconstructionist flippancy belongs to literary critic Gayatri Spivak. Her contempt for British efforts is epitomized by her description of Bentinck's action as "white men saving brown women from brown men."[118] One hastens to explain that this was not so. Indian men such as Roy and Tagore were critical to the abolition movement, and plenty of Indian women enthusiastically supported sati. Spivak imagines that the status of women in Hindu India was the result of collusion between colonialist and nationalist reformers, supported by men of their own predisposition who stood to benefit from their subjugation. As for poor Roop Kanwar, Spivak seems bemused by all the fuss. After all, the teenager may have made an "ethical choice" to become sati. In any case, it is not for western-tainted Indian feminists to pass judgment. And, above all, there must be no collective disavowal of the act, lest it strengthen the prospects of "the very thing we seek to avoid: the virulent misogyny of the Right."[119] Remember, Spivak counsels, "the subaltern cannot speak" so sati is merely the way in which her action was "inscribed on her body."[120] Subsequent police investigation, incidentally, revealed that Roop Kanwar was allowed *no* ethical choice. She "was forcibly dragged . . . and put on the pyre . . . She is said to have screamed and struggled to get out when the pyre was" (miraculously?) "lit, but Rajput youths with swords surrounding her made her escape impossible."[121]

Some Indian scholars also view the legacy of Bentinck in a sinister light, imputing motives far more nefarious than are apparent. Sati, writes one afflicted author, "was, all said, a pathology of colonialism, not of Hinduism. There was almost no sati in the village not exposed to colonialism or among the so-called martial castes."[122] Aside from the obvious point that universality in any respect is rare in India, how then to account for sati's ancient, well-chronicled history, or for its persistence in India even today? "Life goes on, the past continues," Naipaul has explained. "After conquest and destruction" in India "the past simply reasserts itself."[123]

But to the determined Anglophobe, there is little substance to *any* British professions of humanitarian concern. Sati's abolition, like everything the British did in India, was the product of cold, political calculus, designed to assert a state monopoly over the right to take life and to project colonial subjects in a disreputable light, thereby reinforcing the legitimacy of British rule. "The ultimate consideration," sniffs one cynic, "was political."[124] To another, sati "was to be used as a moral justification for Indians to submit to the British Raj," adding, "It became necessary for British writers to SENSATIONALIZE sati on the one hand and for British historians to MONOPOLIZE the credit for having abolished it on the other."[125] Patrick Harrigan of the University of California goes even further. In what can only be described as an exercise in intellectual Ludditism, he veritably rhapsodizes about sati, describing it as voluntary, courageous and "reminiscent of Rajasthan's days of glory." What irritates *him* about the death of Roop Kanwar (above) is the barrage of rabidly anti-sati sentiment "directed by a handful of European-educated proponents of 'social progress'." Harrigan denounces Indian laws against the practice which "appear to be dead-set against sati *in principle*" (author's emphasis), written by elites fond of espousing "foreign principles."[126]

Irrespective of hindsight, the historical record is relatively (and one uses that term advisedly) uncomplicated. Widows were being sacrificed in large numbers, and the governor-general, in the face of mercurial forces impossible wholly to anticipate, stepped in shortly after his arrival to stop it. He was not even in India during the heyday of "surveillance," nor did he collude with grasping Zamindars. The evidence for why Bentinck acted as he did overwhelmingly suggests an explanation which seems all too quaint today: "the possibility that ideas *driven by the process of intellectual discovery* direct our actions by invading our minds."[127] These ideas, then, constituted the basis of the tutelary imperative driving Bentinck and India into the age of westernizing reform.

## DENOUEMENT

The disturbing trends which now obfuscate the record of the British Empire are unsettling in that they confute the historical narrative and then make it conform (through remarkable fancy) to a relativist model that, thereby, is rendered so morally murky as to mean anything, or nothing. One supposes that is the point, to make it impossible to reach objective consensus and draw useful, or in any case acceptable, lessons from the study of history. This relativistic trend is problematic, of course, as it leaves students stranded on the beach, unable to benefit from scrutiny of the past because

> The best they can do is point out all the opinions and cultures there are and have been. What right, they ask, do I or anyone else have to say one is better than the others? If I pose the routine question designed to confute them and make them think, such as "If you had been a British administrator in India, would you let the natives under your governance burn the widow at the funeral of a man who died?", they either remain silent or reply that the British should never have been there in the first place. It is not that they know very much about many other nations, or about their own. The purpose of their education is not to make them scholars but to provide them with a moral virtue—openness.[128]

Perhaps Arthur Hays Sulzberger, longtime publisher of the *New York Times*, was onto something in 1961 when he professed his belief in an open mind, "But not so open that your brains fall out."[129]

The British in India were hardly paragons. Neither could they accurately be labeled inveterate scoundrels. That India had enlightened men such as Bentinck to thank for myriad advantages at independence, unavailable to other emerging nations, there is little doubt. The stark nature of the sati debate provided the humanitarian leverage and philosophical breadth which made further advance possible. By the early nineteenth century, Indian civilization had stopped evolving, its social and political systems grown increasingly exclusive, caste distinctions hardening, reduced to rote formula:

> superstition and fatalism were at a premium . . . Instructions on what, how and where to eat were carried to ludicrous lengths, not only by sophisticated people in the villages, but by the educated elite . . . Excommunication was a deadly weapon, a sword of Damocles hanging over the head of anyone who dared to defy the canons of Hindu Orthodoxy.[130]

Perhaps the time has arrived when even the obvious requires vigorous defending, lest the parameters of the so-called culture wars not merely shift, but transmogrify. Maybe traditional historians have surrendered too much of the debate to the anthropologists, the sociologists, and the literary critics, for in so doing, the rules have changed. We are now living in a time when a scholar can write, without irony, "I believe that ultimately there is no way of writing directly about anything. All *is* a translation or representation of the event."[131] From such a mindset, it is, sadly, a short leap to a world where the issue of widow immolation has two sides (at least), or where reason resides as much in the civilization that so dispatches its widows as in the civilization that does not.

Renowned anthropologist Robert Edgerton has noted the Rousseau-like tradition that folk societies be idealized, even mythologized "to consist of emotional sharing, personal intimacy, moral commitment, social cohesion and continuity over time."[132] He goes on to urge a moratorium on the surviving assumption that the traditional beliefs and proclivities of folk populations are necessarily adaptive while those of modern, westernized societies are not. A better appreciation of all societies' relative adaptiveness will yield an enriched understanding of human adaptation over the course of history.[133] The custom of sati was a maladaptive remnant that required abolition and displacement by the loftier notions embodied in today's Indian constitution, principles which, as with Bentinck and sati, Lincoln and slavery, King and segregation, or Mandela and apartheid, attract the attention of great men and women, and drive humankind forward. And this process accentuates perhaps the most grievous shortcoming of multiculturalist relativism: the paucity of its promise. Sati, and the elites who defended it, were maladaptive for India, which speaks not only to its successful suppression but to the future receptivity of India to "western" ideas. "If we are to understand the processes of cultural adaptation and maladaptation," Edgerton continues

> relativism must be replaced by a form of evaluative analysis. One cannot study the relative success of adaptation without making evaluative judgments. We would never countenance a relativistic prohibition against attempting to evaluate the conditions of life in our inner cities. We know that drug abuse, deteriorated housing, poor prenatal health care, rage and hopelessness are not good for the impoverished and embattled people who live there, and these people know it far better that we do. Why then should the principle of cultural relativism prevent us from evaluating the . . . wife battering " . . . [and widow-burning?] . . . "that exist in many small traditional societies."[134]

That the moral high ground in some circles has been yielded to relativists is itself an indicator of the like tendency among those who should know better than to acquiesce meekly on a principle just as Bentinck's predecessors had so as to avoid unwanted rancor. To resist this temptation, as Edgerton has suggested, is not "to argue that modern urban societies are necessarily better adapted than folk societies . . . ," but, he hastens to add, "in respects such as health, longevity and control of homicide, I believe they are."[135] Yet, "evaluative analysis" presupposes some set of objective standards against which to render a judgment. And such standards do not mystically appear but derive from prevailing traditions, whether home-grown or foreign, which are not only adaptive but also philosophically defensible.

In the end, the main issue becomes a question of the historical record's integrity. If it has none, then the relativists are right after all, and the historian's craft is thereby reduced to an intellectual shell game of esoteric irrelevance. Unless British imperialism in India and elsewhere is appreciated for its successes as well as for its missteps, for its principles alongside its mendacities, for its heroes as well as for its villains, then perspective will be absent in the scholarship and its lessons remain unrevealed and unedifying. This is why it is important to rediscover the British Empire, not so much to answer the rhetorical query as to whether or not it was a "good thing," but to distill from its history an acknowledgment of its positive and negative effects and to minimize the profitless name-calling to which its very existence seems now to have given rise. "It fills me with old nerves to contemplate Indian history," writes V. S. Naipaul, "how close we were to cultural destruction and to wonder at the many accidents which brought us to the concepts—of law and freedom and wide human association which gave men self-awareness and strength . . . "[136] The British in India had arrived at a sort of deliberative, if elitist, universalism with which to resolve issues of fundamental moral conflict between colonizer and colonized without courting political destruction. And in this sense, perhaps, the way was shown toward effective preemption of ethnic conflict today, "away from cultural polarization towards the many multicultural possibilities that are compatible with universal respect for human life, liberty and opportunity."[137] The universalist principles which guided Bentinck are the same ones most likely eventually to bind east and west to each other. In short, British articulation of certain universal philosophic values should be seen as a guarantor of cultural diversity itself. The line between "westernized morality" and integrity of indigenous custom, though necessarily tortuous and equivocal at times, is nonetheless very real and profoundly significant. The empire's "moral sense," was predicated on the "common sense" of its executors.

Since the end of World War II and the emergence of so many independent states out from under the imperial canopy, the tenor of much historical writing has grown brittle, sullen, and, to a large degree, compensatory. Although, as the late Elie Kedourie was at pains to point out, "this (imperial) dominance is now dead and gone . . . both while it lasted and still today it has inspired within the academy sultry and acrid political passions and tenacious political commitments."[138] Acrid indeed, especially if one considers the following passage from a chapter by Tapan Raychaudhuri entitled "British Rule in India: An Assessment" recently published in the *Cambridge Illustrated History of the British Empire*:

> In post-independence India, serious thinkers and historians who see anything good in the imperial record can probably be counted on the fingers of one hand. Even the best known among the persistent admirers of the Raj, Nirad C. Chaudhuri, has described the British in India in the late nineteenth and early twentieth centuries as 'the Nazis of their time.'[139]

Perhaps the moment has arrived to step back, to evaluate the British Empire against the sober and objective standards some historians have consistently maintained and to venture broader perspectives on the imperial role, years after its demise, in man's continuing saga. It should not be left to "the armies of the night to contend over the rights and wrongs of empires."[140] Instead these "rights and wrongs" should be profitably assessed and popularly explicated. Above all, neither scholars nor students should be forced to relive Winston Churchill's conundrum. "We must not mention the Empire," he once admonished a crowd, "it's naughty."

## REFERENCES

1. Sir Penderel Moon, *The British Conquest and Dominion of India* (London: Duckworth, 1989), 577.
2. John Buchan, *Memory Hold the Door* (London: Hadden and Sloughton Ltd., 1940), 124–125.
3. Edward Said, *Culture and Imperialism* (New York: Knopf, 1993), 5.
4. Brigitte Berger, "Multiculturalism and the Modern University", from Edith Kurzweil and William Philips, eds., *Our Country, Our Culture: The Politics of Political Correctness* (New York: Partisan Review Press, 1994), 21.
5. Bernard Lewis, *Race and Slavery in the Middle East: A Historical Enquiry* (Oxford: Oxford Univ. Press, 1990), 99.
6. Alan Bloom, *The Closing of the American Mind* (New York: Simon and Schuster, 1987), 39–40.

7. Eric Stokes, *English Utilitarians and India* (Oxford: Clarendon Press, 1959), 31.
8. Orlando Patterson, *Freedom* (New York: Basic Books, 1991), 402–403. Cited in James Q. Wilson, *The Moral Sense* (New York: Free Press, 1993), 195.
9. John Stuart Mill, Bentham in Dissertations and Discussions 2 Vols. (London, 1858) Vol. I, 337. Cited in Surash Chandra Ghosh, "The Utilitarianism of Dalhousie" *Modern Asian Studies*, 12, 1 (1978), 102.
10. J. Majeed, "James Mill's 'The History of British India' and Utilitarianism as a Rhetoric of Reform," *Modern Asian Studies*, 24, 2 (1990), 223–224.
11. Donald E. Smith, *India as a Secular State* (Princeton: Princeton Univ. Press, 1963), 217.
12. Percival Griffiths *The British Impact on India* (Hamden, Connecticut: Archon Press) 1965, 217.
13. Philip Woodruff, *The Men Who Ruled India*, Vol. I (London: Jonathan Cape, 1954), 254.
14. Arvind Sharma, et al., *Sati: Historical and Phenomenological Essays* (Delhi: Motilal Banarsidass, 1988), 86n.
15. R. C. Majumdar, ed., *British Paramountcy and Indian Renaissance* Part II (Bombay: Bharatiya Vidya Bhavan, 1965), 269–270.
16. Robert Charles Zaehner, *Hinduism* (New York: Oxford Univ. Press, 1966), 112.
17. Majumdar, 269.
18. Iqbal Singh, *Rammohun Roy* (Bombay: Asia Publishing House, 1958), 191.
19. Woodruff, 253. Cited in Edward Thompson and G. T. Garratt. *The Rise and Fulfillment of British Rule in India* (Allahabad: Central Book Depot 1962) p. 326. Philip Woodruff is a pseudonym for Philip Mason, an Indian civil servant who later reissued his works and published others under his real name.
20. Singh, 193.
21. William Foster, Ed., *Early Travels in India, 1583–1619* (London: Oxford Univ. Press, 1921), 220.
22. Sharma, 88.
23. Thompson and Garratt, 327.
24. Thompson and Garratt, 327–328.
25. Sakuntala Narasimhan, *Sati: A Study of Widow Burning in India* (New Delhi: Viking, 1990), 67.
26. Narasimhan, 67.
27. Narasimhan, 63–65.
28. Pegg, *India's Cries to British Humanity* (2nd Ed., 1830), 14. Cited in Thompson and Garratt, 328.
29. A. C. Lyle, "Our Religious Policy in India," *Fortnightly Review*, April, 1872, 388–389. Cited in Smith, 68.
30. Mulk Raj Anand, *Sati* (Delhi: B.R. Publishing, 1989), 3.
31. Woodruff, 258.
32. Woodruff, 257–258.
33. Clive Dewey, *Anglo-Indian Attitudes: The Mind of the Indian Civil Service* (London: Hambledon Press, 1993), preface, vii–viii.
34. Woodruff, 259.

35. Anand, 3. Both Robert Clive, the victor at Plassey and Warren Hastings, an East India Company Governor-General, were severely criticized in England for corruption and self-enrichment while in India. Hastings was acquitted after impeachment in the House of Commons by an reformist faction including both Charles James Fox and the great parliamentarian Edmund Burke.

36. Demetrius Boulger, *Lord William Bentinck* (Oxford: Clarendon Press, 1897), 85–86.

37. Boulger, 84.

38. Marshman 1867:52. Cited in Hanne Georgeson, "Representations of Hindu Women Through Some of the Rewritings on Widow-Burning," *The Australian Journal of Anthropology*, Vol. 3: 3 (Fall 1992), 160.

39. Marshman, 161.

40. Marshman, 166.

41. Narasimhan, 63–65.

42. Georgeson, 166.

43. Narasimhan, 65.

44. Extract from official records relating to sati, 1822. Cited in Narasimhan, 61.

45. Majumdar, 271.

46. Lord Amherst's *Minute on Suttee*, 18 March 1827, Majumdar, 1941, cited in Georgeson, 167.

47. Griffiths, 245.

48. Ram Gopal, *British Rule in India, An Assessment* (New York: Asia Publishing House, 1963), 117–118.

49. Griffiths, 246.

50. K. M. Pannikar, *Hindu Society at Cross Roads* (Bombay: Asia Publishing House, 1955), 41. Cited in Smith, 217.

51. Griffiths, 217.

52. James Q. Wilson, *The Moral Sense* (New York: The Free Press, 1993), 239.

53. Dewey, vii–viii.

54. Stokes, 249.

55. Boulger, 94–95.

56. Boulger, 78. Thugee was a cult practice of robbery and ritual murder (usually strangulation) of travellers centered around the goddess Kali which accounted for the deaths of thousands along the byways of India until suppressed by the British early in the nineteenth century.

57. Boulger, 17.

58. Boulger, 35–36.

59. Boulger, 37.

60. Bentinck to Col. Young, 28 Dec 1827, Bentham, *Works X*, 576–578, cited in Stokes, 51.

61. Geoffrey Moorhouse, *India Britannica* (New York: Harper and Row, 1983), 91.

62. Moon, 450.

63. Minutes (Mil. Dept.), 20 Jan. 1835 BP/PW Jb/25, PW Jf/2910, cited in Rosselli, 217.

64. Bentinck Minute, 4 Feb. 1834, No. 2902, cited in Rosselli, *Lord William Bentinck*, 216.

65. Bentinck to Money, 1 June 1834, No. 2643/i—quoted in Perceval Spear

*Lord William Bentinck*, 109–110. *Dictionary of National Biography* ii, 292–297.

66. Moorhouse, 92.
67. Moon, 451.
68. C. H. Philips, Ed. *The Correspondence of Lord William Cavendish Bentinck, Governor-General of India 1828–1835 V. I* (Oxford: Oxford Univ. Press, 1977), Intro. xxviii.
69. Wilson, 215.
70. Boulger, 87.
71. Kalides Naq, ed. *The English Works of Rammohun Roy*, 1947. Cited in Ajit Kumar Ray, *Widows Are Not for Burning* (New Delhi: ABC Publishing, 1985), 40.
72. Moorhouse, 85, 86. Philip Mason has remarked that while many enlightened Indians came to denounce sati, "to the old-fashioned and orthodox it was an attack on religion. It was remembered." Philip Mason *A Matter of Honor An Account of the Indian Army Its Officers and Men* (Middlesex, England: Penguin Books), 1974. p. 260. Another historian has noted that most of the sepoys in Company service were recruited in North India, where sati was rare. John Rosselli, *Lord William Bentinck* p. 214.
73. Smith, 69.
74. Blair B. Kling, *Partner in Empire* (Berkeley: Univ. of California Press, 1976), 23.
75. Kalides Nag and Debajyoti Burman, eds., *The English Works of Rammohun Roy, Part III* (Calcutta: Sadharan Brahmo Samaj, 1946, 136, cited in S. Crawford, *Ram Mohan Roy: Social, Political and Religious Reform in Nineteenth Century India* (New York: Paragon House, 1987), 113–114.
76. V. S. Naipaul, *India: A Million Mutinies Now* (New York: Penguin, 1990), 286.
77. T. O. Lloyd, *The British Empire 1538–1983* (New York: Oxford Univ. Press, 1984), 150.
78. Boulger, 96.
79. Boulger, 97.
80. Boulger, 98.
81. Boulger, 100.
82. Boulger, 102. Permanent Settlement was a system of revenue collection inaugurated by Lord Cornwallis in 1793 in an effort to establish a landed aristocracy on the old Whig model to lend stability to Bengal. Instead, the system resulted in the ascendancy of a moneylending class of absentee landlords who displaced traditional landowners, resulting in widespread peasant dispossession.
83. Boulger, 104, 109.
84. Boulger, 110–111.
85. Griffiths, 215.
86. V. N. Datta, *Sati* (London: Sangam Books, 1983), 80.
87. Marshman, 413. Cited in Datta, 80.
88. Narasimham, 70.
89. Woodruff, 258–259.
90. Woodruff, 258–259.
91. Sachchidananda Bhattacharya, *A Dictionary of Indian History* (Calcutta: Univ. of Calcutta Press, 1967), 755.

92. *Up the Country*, 310. Cited in Thompson and Garratt, 342.
93. Quoted from *Raja R. M. Roy and Progressive Movements in India: A Selection form the Records, 1775–1785*, 157. In David Kopf, *British Orientalism and the Bengal Renaissance. The Dynamics of Indian Modernization 1773–1785* (Berkeley: Univ. of California Press, 1969), p. 270.
94. Philips, 367.
95. From the *Asiatic Journal*, N.S., vol. II, Asiatic Intelligence, 189, qtd in Anand, Appendix 3, 72n.
96. Anand, Appendix 2, 69–70.
97. Pramatha Nath Bose, *A History of Hindu Civilization during British Rule*, v. II (Calcutta: W. Newman and Co., 1894), 81. Cited in Anand, Appendix 2, 81n.
98. Sharma, 46.
99. Phillips, 349.
100. Edward Thompson, *Suttee* (London: George Allen and Unwin, 1928), 77–78.
101. From a pamphlet entitled "Vindications of the Hindus, by a Bengal Officer" cited in Moorhouse, 89.
102. P. J. Marshall, ed., *The British Discovery of Hinduism in the Eighteenth Century* (Cambridge: Cambridge Univ. Press, 1970), 95–96, cited in Sharma, 90–91n.
103. A. Yusuf Ali, *A Cultural History of India During the British Period* (New York: AMS Press, 1940), Preface vi.
104. Sharma, 92n.
105. Vivekananda, *The Complete Works of Swami Vivekananda*, vol. III (Calcutta: Advaita Ashram, 1960), 506, cited in Sharma, p. 93n.
106. P. V. Kane, *History of Dharmasastra*, vol. I (Calcutta: Bhandarkar Oriental Research Institute, 1941), 636, cited in Sharma, p. 99n.
107. Salamat Ail, "A Young Widow Burns in Her Bridal Clothes", *Far Eastern Economic Review* No. 138 (Oct. 8, 1987), 54–55. Other estimates placed the crowd size at over 300,000 (Edgerton, *Sick Societies*, 138).
108. Cited in H. C. Upreti and Nandini Upreti, *The Myth of Sati* (Bombay: Himalaya Publishing, 1991), 102.
109. Woodruff, 258.
110. P. V. Kane, 636, cited in Upreti and Upreti, 101.
111. Georgeson, 171.
112. Georgeson, 162.
113. Georgeson, 158–159.
114. Georgeson, 170.
115. Nancy L. Paxton, "Disembodied Subjects: English Women's autobiography Under the Raj." From Sidonie Smith and Julia Watson, eds., *Decolonizing the Subject* (Minneapolis: Univ. of Minnesota Press, 1992), 390.
116. Dorothy Stein, "Burning Widows, Burning Brides: The Perils of Daughterhood in India," *Pacific Affairs*, No. 61 (Fall 1988), 465–485.
117. John Leonard, "Novel Colonies" (review) *The Nation* (March 22, 1993), 384.
118. Georgeson, 151–152.
119. Donna Landry and Gerald MacLean, eds., *The Spivak Reader* (New York: Routledge, 1996), 252.
120. Landry and MacLean, 289.

121. *Trial By Fire, A Report on Roop Kanwar's Death* (Bombay: Women and Media Committee, Bombay Union of Journalists).

122. Anand, Addendum X, 158–159.

123. V. S. Naipaul, *India: A Wounded Civilization* (New York: Vintage, 1978), 6.

124. Narasimhan, 141–142.

125. Sharma, 10.

126. Patrick Harrigan "Tyranny of the Elect?" *The Statesman*. vol. 122: 25688 (Nov. 3, 1987).

127. Dewey, Preface viii. Zamindars were large landowners-cum-tax collectors who both insured payment of requisite revenues to the ruler while retaining whatever he could squeeze from the peasant cultivators.

128. Alan Bloom, *The Closing of the American Mind* (New York: Simon and Schuster, 1987), 26.

129. *New York Times*, 29 July 1996, A11.

130. B. R. Nanda, *Gokhale, The Indian Moderates and the British Raj* (Princeton: Princeton Univ. Press, 1977), 72–73.

131. Georgeson, 152.

132. Robert B. Edgerton, *Sick Societies, Challenging the Myth of Primitive Harmony* (New York: Macmillan, 1992), 205.

133. Edgerton, 204–205.

134. Edgerton, 207.

135. Edgerton, 204.

136. V. S. Naipaul, *India: A Million Mutinies Now*, 398–399.

137. Amy Gutmann, "The Challenge of Multiculturalism in Political Ethics," *Philosophy and Public Affairs* v. 22, 3, Summer 1993, 206.

138. Elie Kedourie, "Politics and the Academy," *Commentary* 94 August 1992, 53.

139. Nirad C. Chaudhuri quoted by Tapan Raychaudhuri in P. J. Marshall, ed., *The Cambridge Illustrated History of the British Empire* (Cambridge: Cambridge Univ. Press, 1996), 358.

140. Lawrence James, *The Rise and Fall of the British Empire* (New York: St. Martin's Press, 1994), Introduction, XV.

# SELECTED BIBLIOGRAPHY


Bayly, Christopher. *Imperial Meridian: The British Empire and the World 1780–1830* (1989).

Cain, P. J. and Hopkins, A. G. *British Imperialism: Innovation and Expansion 1688–1914* (London: Longman).

*Cambridge Illustrated History of the British Empire*, ed. P. J. Marshall (Cambridge: Cambridge Univ. Press, 1996).

Colley, Linda. *Britons: Forging the Nation* (New Haven, CT, and London: Yale Univ. Press, 1992).

Darwin, John. *Britain and Decolonisation: The Retreat from Empire in the Post-War World* (New York: St. Martin's, 1988).

Hobsbawn, E. J. *The Age of Empire 1875–1914* (New York: Vintage, 1986).

——. *Empire and Sexuality: The British Experience* (Manchester: Manchester Univ. Press, 1990).

James, Lawrence. *The Rise and Fall of the British Empire* (London: Abacus, 1994).

Judd, Denis. *Empire: The British Imperial Experience from 1765 to the Present* (New York: Basic Books, 1996).

Louis, W. Roger. *The British Empire in the Middle East 1945–51* (Oxford: Oxford Univ. Press, 1984).

Marshall, P. J. *Bengal: the British Bridgehead: Eastern India 1740–1828* (1987).

Monroe, Elizabeth. *Britain's Moment in the Middle East, 1914–1956* (Baltimore: Johns Hopkins Press, 1963).

Porter, A. N. *European Imperialism, 1860–1914* (Hampshire, England: Macmillan, 1994).

Prakash, Gyan. *After Colonialism: Imperial Histories and Postcolonial Displacements* (Princeton, NJ: Princeton Univ. Press, 1995).

Said, Edward W. *Culture and Imperialism* (London: Vintage, 1994).

# SELECTED BIBLIOGRAPHY

# INDEX